THOUGHT CATALOG BOOKS

Beyond Anxiety

Beyond Anxiety

Essays About Panic, Worry, And Finding Healing

THOUGHT CATALOG

THOUGHT CATALOG BOOKS

Brooklyn, NY

THOUGHT CATALOG BOOKS

Copyright © 2016 by The Thought & Expression Co.

All rights reserved. Published by Thought Catalog Books, a division of The Thought & Expression Co., Williamsburg, Brooklyn. Founded in 2010, Thought Catalog is a website and imprint dedicated to your ideas and stories. We publish fiction and non-fiction from emerging and established writers across all genres. For general information and submissions: manuscripts@thoughtcatalog.com.

First edition, 2016

ISBN 978-1540307057

10 9 8 7 6 5 4 3 2 1

Cover design by © KJ Parish

Contents

1

What Is Anxiety?

Sachinee Seneviratne

Anxiety disorder does not mean getting anxious the night before a big game or an interview. It's not the nervousness you feel before an exam. It's a constant and exhausting cycle of your thoughts telling you that you're no good.

Sometimes I'm not even aware of what I'm anxious about. All I know is that I am worried. This worrying keeps me paralyzed in my room for days. It stops me from doing the things I love and makes me disinterested in everything.

Then there are days where I'm less anxious, where I go out and about trying to make the best of the little time I have for myself. I know it will be back, though. I know this is a gift I've been given that could be taken away at any time.

My earliest memory of anxiety was when I was eight. I'd stay up half the night, thinking I would die if I fell asleep. That isn't the kind of irrational fear that should run through the mind of an eight year old, but I was not aware of that. I wouldn't tell anyone about this either because I believed it would go away.

I guess that specific thought eventually did, but only to be replaced with other paranoid thoughts. No matter what I did, my anxiety kept bothering me throughout the years.

I know it's not easy. In fact, it's far from it. It's carrying demons on your shoulders everywhere you go. They whisper things in your ear that you don't want to listen to. They tell you that you're not good enough and that you shouldn't even try. Your thoughts defy reality, yet you listen to them and let them bring you down.

Having anxiety is not wanting to go out in public because you do not know when your next attack will be. It's living in fear that you will not have a safe place to calm yourself down. It's getting swarmed by tears that you can't stop. It's fear that runs through your head all day and all night, even when you know it has no real base.

Anxiety blows all of my paranoid thoughts out of proportion and makes a needle look like an ax. My anxiety cannot be seen and it cannot be heard by others, so I'm probably overreacting, right? *Wrong.* It is as real as diabetes and cancer. If I told you the number of times a day I had thought about killing myself, just to get the thoughts to stop, you would be shocked.

It took me thirteen years to learn how to get these demons to sit next to me. To invite them over for tea and ask them why they're doing this. To find out how we got here. I know I should have done this years ago, but I didn't realize crippling anxiety created the demons on my shoulders. I mistook them for depression. I didn't know they came together for me, like a pair of gloves. One not sold without the other.

My anxiety tells me I'm not good enough, not smart enough, not loved enough. That anybody who decides to love me will eventually change their mind and all the happiness I feel in that rare moment will be taken away from me. I cannot count the number of times I've told myself it's going to be fine over and over again or the number of times I've had to take a breath in and hold it for a few seconds just to feel slightly less anxious.

I know it's in my head, but you need to know that I, without question, cannot control it. If I could, I would have already. Believe me, torturing myself isn't on my list of favorite things to do.

Now I know where these demons come from, and instead of being afraid of them, I have become friends with them. We sit side by side and they let me go through my day. Yes, they do try to stop me sometimes, but I know how to control them.

I don't know if I can ever get them to leave, but I know my anxiety was my greatest teacher to date, and I will eternally be grateful for the things it has made me realize and for the people who have loved me through this exhausting process.

The best part is, once I get through this, I'll have a story to tell. I'll come out stronger on the other side, and more difficult to beat.

2

10 Things That Happen When You're Fighting A Battle No One Knows About

Rania Naim

1. You feel all alone even in a big group. You feel disconnected from everyone around you, you can be talking and having great conversations but still feel like no one really gets you or understands what you're trying to say. You're more likely to listen than talk because it's *easier* this way.

2. People will give you all sorts of labels. They'll call you *'moody'* or *'unpredictable'* or *'distant,'* but that's mainly because some days are better than others and no one really knows what's happening inside you.

3. You tried to talk about it but nothing changed. You talked to your friends, your family and maybe your therapist about it but it's still a challenge to explain what you're going through. *Sometimes even the wisest person won't understand what's happening to you until it happens to them.*

4. You're tired of pretending you're okay. You're tired of saying there is nothing wrong with you when there is, you're tired of having to lie to people about what's going on and you're tired of pretending to be strong and smiling when all you want to do is cry. You wish you could just let everyone know what's wrong with you so they can leave you alone but you know that's not possible.

5. You're more guarded. You're not as open and friendly as you used to be. You're cautious with everything because you don't want anyone to make your battles worse. People mistake you for being aloof when the truth is you're just trying to *protect* yourself.

6. You're easily disappointed. When you're fighting a battle no one knows about, the smallest thing can put a damper on your mood and trigger negative emotions. You're easily hurt by the slightest remarks or even jokes just to give yourself the right to get mad at something.

7. Your mind is perplexed. You're easily distracted, you're forgetful and you always feel like there is just not enough hours in the day to do everything you've been wanting to do. You're always stressed out and you're always anxious—even in your *sleep*.

8. You feel like you need isolation. You think the more you participate in real life, the more you screw up. You feel like you need a vacation, somewhere far away—*away* from people and away from *noise* to *piece* yourself together again.

9. You keep praying but you're losing hope. You keep praying for things to get better, for things to change but part of you feels like that's something that will stay with you because you don't know how to shake it off and you don't know if anyone can help you with it.

10. You know you're the only one who can help yourself but you're still trying to figure out *how.*

3

Stop Acting Like Mental Illness Is Cute And Trendy—It's Literally The Opposite

Jessica Wilson

If anxiety was trendy, why don't people understand it? If it's cool to sit at work and watch your thoughts run away from you, or barely bring ourselves to get up for work in the first place, why are people so entitled to change the subject (or worse, not talk at all) when you speak on that black cloud that's always above your head? Why did it become a fad to self-diagnose very real disorders that very real people deal with every day?

I want to make it clear that I am speaking on behalf of everyone with a mental illness that has a stigma attached to it. I'm speaking on behalf of those with medical records in a psychiatric center or documentation of a diagnosis from a psychologist for manic depression, acute anxiety, borderline personality disorder, and on behalf of the mother who gave birth to her baby and cried for 3 weeks straight, to find out on their first month check up, that she scored high enough on that survey to go see a doctor that specializes in postpartum depression. I am not speaking on behalf of the people who have a bad day and then label themselves depressed. I am not speaking on behalf of the people who have a tidy home and call themselves OCD; because chances are, you don't count the shelves twice or turn the lamp on and off and on and off…

And on. And off again. Count to 12. That's 13, that's bad luck, start over. You need an even number. On, off, on, off, on off… and then you try not to scream because you're so fucking frustrated that it still doesn't feel right and you just wish this would go away and you didn't have to the lock the door 7 times before leaving the house or count the cracks in the sidewalks when you finally manage to get outside.

Our world is torn between shunning those who have a mental illness, and dressing up our personalities with a diagnosis we know little to nothing about.

I know way too many people prescribed Xanax and take it every day and prescribed a serotonin inhibitor and take it three times a week and wonder why they're so miserable. I encourage them to know more about their diagnosis, and even more about how these medications work.

I also know way too many people that complain about how bad their anxiety is but can't tell me what's life to have your chest hurt and your mind go blank and sit in the last stall and cry because you lost your shit in the middle of the work day, for no reason other than your dad wouldn't text you back.

Car accident, he's disappointed, your sister got hurt, grandma or grandpa died, he's tired of you living at home and he will probably tell you it's time to leave when you get there.

I'm not here to denounce anyone who talks about their issues. I'm just here to stand up for those of us who don't- because it isn't that easy. Maybe I'm here to tell people to stop throwing around words like anxiety and depression and wearing them as an accessory. I just want to know when this became glamorous. I want to applaud the person prescribed Xanax that takes it when they know they're about to lose it.

And then doesn't touch it again until the next time they are in a crowd of people and feels like every single person is looking at them the wrong way.

I want to talk to the person who offers theirs to the recovering addict who "needs it to feel better" but refuses to see a doctor. I want to ask them why, and I want to tell them to stop.

But you can't affect free will.

I've had the same people who scoffed at my suicide attempt tweet things like "I hate dealing with anxiety." Maybe a selfie with the caption "Anxiety sucks." I can't understand the point of making fun of me for my struggles and then broadcasting your own in a completely unrelated picture. You're smiling, you're laughing, you felt good about yourself today, and you probably only took that picture one time before you decided it was worthy enough for social media.

This is where it becomes unfair for people to throw these things around. Anxiety and depression are everything but confident. Well, maybe not all. Sometimes being manic depressive is a little different. Maybe one day, you feel like you're Beyonce and the next day, you are on the verge of tears with shaking hands wondering why you aren't good enough and no one wants to be your friend. Instead of taking a picture in the mirror, you're standing in front of it wondering if anyone would like you better if you cut your hair, or lost weight, or didn't talk as much or talked even more because at least you'd know how to carry on a conversation.

Mental illness doesn't need to be worn like this season's jeans. Mental illness is not an eyeshadow you put on every single day but don't wear on others. Mental illness is not the lipstick you put on when it's Saturday and need an excuse to drink excessively. You don't wake up and decide you have acute anxiety or OCD or bipolar disorder. You wake up and you put your feet on the floor, take your medicine and you pray to God you have a good day today.

And then, you grab your purse, put on your lipstick and pray even harder that today, the workings of your mind won't take you away from yourself. You pray that today, you can smile without having to cry.

4

6 Things The Internet Gets Wrong About Mental Illness (From Someone With An Anxiety Disorder)

Chelsea Fagan

Well, I suppose it's a good a time as any to formally announce it: I have anxiety. Yes, like "a doctor told me and I take some medication (though not benzos)"-style clinical anxiety. I don't really talk about it because, well, I'd like to hope that it doesn't qualify as part of what I have to offer the world. It's something that I work to manage, and hopefully one day overcome entirely. I have always felt this way, but it appears that the internet—with its endless stream of comics and articles and Tumblr slideshows about how to treat people with mental illness—does not feel that way. And here, the things I think the internet gets most egregiously wrong about people like me.

1. "How to love someone with _____" wildly misses the point.

Few things make me more upset than seeing articles/cartoons about "How to love someone with anxiety" or "How to love someone with depression." Ummm, how about maybe we are not ready to be in a relationship with another person if we are still at the point where this other person would need a Power-Point presentation of special rules to deal with us? The truth is that relationships are a privilege and require two people who can equally give to the equation, and the person with the mental illness does not deserve a bunch of special treatment (but the significant other *does* deserve someone who can be emotionally present at all times). Sometimes our illness makes romantic relationships impossible, and we have an enormous amount of work ahead of us if we want to be able to share our lives with someone.

2. There are degrees of illness, and we're not all the same.

I know where I fit on the spectrum. I am much better than I used to be (at one point I was compulsively lying and picking at my skin, which was just sExY aS hElL!!), but I've never been truly handicapped by my illness. I am able to function in society, and, for the most part, hide my problems. While the symptoms are occasionally physical, I am not as far along as other people who have seizure-like attacks or who can't leave their home—nowhere close. And when we paint ourselves with this brush of "mentally ill," it erases an enormous amount of variation on the spectrum that is incredibly important. Part of the reason I don't like to talk about these issues myself is because I know how lucky I am and that people who are truly disabled in society should take priority in the conversation. Some of us, if we're being honest with ourselves, can emotionally bootstrap and make it work on a day-to-day basis. And that is HUGELY important to acknowledge.

3. Asking people to accommodate illness can be deeply selfish.

I grew up in a household with a parent who suffered from mental illness. I remember the highs and lows, the good days and the bad days, and praying on a regular basis that they would magically get better—because I was afraid that I was causing the problem. Through years of hard work, therapy, medication, and lifestyle change, the illness is not conquered—it never truly is, of course—but it is manageable and, in day-to-day life, not noticeable. But on the worst of the bad days, it became a problem that overtook the family, that made a simple trip to the store or little league game an enormous undertaking. And while I don't resent it, in the moment, it was incredibly difficult for everyone around the mentally ill person. This is something we don't remember enough: While we may be battling severe depression, or obsessive-compulsive disorder, or anxiety attacks, the people who love us (or are even just around us) are suffering, as well. Sometimes, people cannot handle this, and if they choose to leave our lives for *their own* mental health, that is something we have to accept.

4. While mental illness is not something to be ashamed of, it's not something to be proud of, either. It just is.

Mistaking a disorder for a personality trait is truly the worst, and if you are listing it first in your online bios, you should probably consider everything else you have going on in your life, and what you have to offer the world.

5. Learning to live in everyone else's world is a daily game.

I often see articles about "if you need space, you just take it," or "if you can't go to this party, or see that person, don't do it." The idea is that all of these social obligations are constructs, and if they interfere with our mental health, we should be able to drop them. And we can. But the people around you—employers, friends, lovers—have just as much a right to say these things to you. If you are the person who is constantly breaking plans at the last minute because you are overwhelmed at the idea of leaving your apartment, that is something you have to work your hardest to overcome. The onus is on us to become a functioning, empathetic, generous member of our social groups and society in general, not the other way around. If we indulge our illness at every turn and find ourselves alone, we know who to blame for this. I had to recently stop reaching out to a person because she would take days to respond and say "Sorry, I wasn't in a headspace to message you back. Been just holed up at the apartment." And that doesn't make me a bad person.

6. Other people are having trouble, too.

No matter how sick we are, the people around us won't magically have it easier in comparison. Even if someone is mentally "healthy," their life can still be fraught with problems and external factors that are causing them any number of symptoms. Positioning ourselves as the group that needs to be constantly accommodated, because we are the "sick" ones, is both selfish and unproductive. Everyone is having a hard time. Everyone is dealing with something. And we are not special for having a brain that works a little differently than others, we are people that need to participate in this great societal ecosystem. We should have enormous empathy and patience for others, if we expect it for ourselves. We don't just get to be an asshole because of our personal problems, no matter how satisfying it can be. (AND YES, THAT GOES FOR YOU, TOO, INTROVERTS.)

5

What It's Like To Grow Up With Anxiety

Ari Eastman

Anxiety was the first thing I learned belonged to me. Even before my voice or body, or a killer DVD collection (including every season of *Buffy The Vampire Slayer*), Anxiety made her presence known. She was mine, and I was hers—some sick symbiotic relationship. There were days I wasn't even sure I'd know who I was without her.

Anxiety was the girl I hung out with on the blacktop. She'd wait for me at the bottom of the slide, hung around on the monkey bars while I was goofing around with my peers. She made sure I knew she wasn't going anywhere.

She found cracks in every building, imperfections in every foundation. During class, she'd whisper facts about earthquakes—like how more than 80% of San Francisco was destroyed as a result of the 1902 quake. She'd toy with me, distracting me from the tasks at hand. She thought it much better I focus on other things, like fear.

The first time I had a panic attack, I thought I was dying.

And I don't mean that to be hyperbolic. I *literally* thought I was dying.

Anxiety likes to do that. She doesn't ever want you settling in. She doesn't want you to feel comfortable for too long.

The older I got, the more I learned the way I felt wasn't normal. But that didn't mean I was abnormal either. **Nearly 18% of the U.S. population suffer from anxiety disorders.** So, I wasn't alone. Even if, growing up, I was convinced I was.

I thought Anxiety had picked me, *specifically* me. It was my burden to bear. I thought I was the only kid who felt stressed out when no immediate danger was present.

Mental illnesses do a good job at convincing you that you'll never be understood. When the reality is, so, so many people out there are struggling just like you are. You just can't always see it.

To any young person (or really, any age) feeling alone with their anxiety right now, I promise, you're not. It may seem like Anxiety belongs to you, and only you, but there are people out there who are going through the same thing.

Anxiety is not easy. It's not a characteristic of a one-dimensional sitcom character. It's not something that makes sense. But when we share our experiences, we grow together.

Anxiety may have been the first thing I learned belonged to

me, but I now know it's not all. It's just a facet. It's just a tiny part.

6

10 Ways Anxiety Has Affected My Life

Erin Critelli

Do you ever worry so much that you cannot sleep at night? Do you feel that people are always judging you? Anxiety is an illness that many people suffer from on a daily basis and the dark places that it can leave you in are scary. These are the reasons it has affected my life.

1. Before going to a party or huge event I become nervous, I say to myself, "Will everyone like me, do they like me?"

2. The thoughts of paranoia keep me up at night and I find myself tossing and turning till I am so tired that I eventually fall asleep.

3. I constantly worry if others like me or if they are judging me, it is almost like I am obsessed with that frame of thinking.

4. "I'm sorry." Why do I always have to say I am sorry? Even for something I did not do or have any control over. I always feel the need to express my sympathies because God forbid that person does not like me anymore. How crazy is that?

5. OMG someone did not like my Instagram post! Really? Who cares, but I do… somehow my mind goes to that low point that if someone does not like my social media post that they no longer like me anymore.

6. Shit, they haven't texted me back yet, but it has been a few hours! Hmm… I guess they do not want to answer me. "Did I ever think maybe they were busy?" No, of course not, because it would be too easy to think that way.

7. I can never say no because I do not want to make anyone mad or upset. But, what about my life? My feelings?

8. I have always allowed others to walk all over me, it is wrong, but I still allow it.

9. I am always worried about when I am going to get my career and when I am going to be financially stable instead of trying to take each day one step at a time.

10. I always worry so much about other people in my life that I forget who I am as a person and I lose out on taking care of myself.

Living each day with anxiety is painful and frustrating. As much as my loved ones tell me there is no need to worry about that, I still do anyway. It is a struggle each and every day; *I encourage those who do find themselves with anxiety to please get help.* It is not something that can be taken lightly.

7

11 Things People Don't Realize You Are Doing Because Of Your Anxiety

Lauren Jarvis-Gibson

1. Decline invites even when you really want to go.

Sometimes, anxiety can be so debilitating, that you can't muster enough energy to go out. No matter how excited you were for the event beforehand, when the day actually comes and your anxiety is in full force, you say no. You don't want to be a burden to anyone if you were to go, so the best choice for you is to not attend.

2. Obsess over things people normally would never think about twice.

You obsess over *everything* in your head. Most likely, the things you obsess about would never cross someone's mind who doesn't have anxiety. Maybe you obsess over a conversation you had last week or the way your boss looked at you the other day. Maybe you obsess over the fact that your boyfriend hasn't texted you in a day, and you worry if you said anything to upset him. Whatever it may be, it's hard for people without anxiety to understand why you are so caught up in things that wouldn't even matter to them.

3. Wake up early in the morning even when you're tired.

Sleep is always an issue for you. It's hard for you to get to sleep because you have so many things to digest and contemplate about the day you just had. Because your mind never seems to shut off, you never fail to wake up early with worries that have already entered your mind. You tend to wake up super early sometimes because you need to get going and get everything done in a timely manner. Sleeping in is definitely a challenge for you because you can't switch off your anxiety once you are already awake.

4. You constantly fear the worst scenario in every situation.

Before first dates, you are convinced it's going to go terribly wrong. Before going on a trip, you envision everything falling apart. Before going on a road trip, you fear accidents. When you get sick, you get terrified that there's something truly wrong with you. The list goes on and on, and it seems silly to others. But for you? It's real fears. It's real to you.

5. You replay conversations over and over in your head.

You try to avoid confrontation at all costs because it causes your anxiety to get worse. When you have an argument or even a conversation that seems lovely to the other person, you continue to think about it after it's said and done. You can never get it out of your head and you *always* think you said something wrong. It can really eat you up inside, and you always have to remind yourself that it's just your anxiety talking, and everything is most likely fine.

6. You become more worried for yourself when people voice concern for you.

When people ask you if you are ok when you are having an anxiety attack, or when people come to you when you are way over your head with negative thoughts, it makes your anxiety worse. Of course, they all mean well, but when others worry for you, it makes you think – "If *they* are worried, then I should worry even more about myself!"

7. You think it's your fault when someone doesn't reply right away.

Whether it's your significant other, your best friend, or sister, you constantly get worked up when people don't respond to you. People without anxiety would usually not pay it any mind, but for you, it's a huge deal. Usually when people don't answer you or text you back, you think that it's all of your fault. You always think that you did something wrong, when most likely, they are just terrible at communication.

8. You sometimes feel like you are having a breakdown every few days when mention of the future is brought up.

The future is a huge trigger for you. You hate when people ask you what your plans are for the next five years, and it will cause you to retreat. Graduating from high school and college for most people is very exciting, but for you, it can be incredibly daunting and scary. You hate when people talk about their own future because it makes you feel like you aren't good enough.

9. You constantly compare your success to other people who are the same age as you.

You constantly see on Facebook that people your own age are getting their dream jobs, and it makes your head want to explode. You don't want to compare yourself to others, but sometimes your anxiety gets the best of you and you can't help it. You worry if you are ever going to measure up to them and if your goals are ever going to come true.

10. You replay every mistake you make, and always beat yourself up over it.

Especially if you make a mistake at work, it can consume your thoughts and can ruin your day, or even week. You constantly strive to do the best that you can do, but when you accidentally send something that you shouldn't, or when you do something you weren't supposed to do in the office, you can get really down on yourself. Anxiety can truly be your worst enemy.

11. On some days you are too physically and mentally exhausted to get out of bed.

Some days, your anxiety can be so strong, that you truly feel unable to do anything but lie in bed and cry. At times, the world can be way too much for your mind to handle, and you'll need to take a few days off and rest your mind and tired body. Anxiety can have a huge effect on our health, and it is not something to brush off to the side. It can be truly harmful, and a lot of people don't understand the effects it can have on an individual.

8

15 Things You Need To Know About People Who Have Concealed Anxiety

Brianna Wiest

1. They don't hide their anxiety, they hide their symptoms. To have concealed anxiety isn't to deny having it—only to do everything in your power to ensure other people don't see you struggle.

2. They have the most anxiety about having anxiety. Because they are not comfortable letting people see them in the throes of an irrational panic, the most anxiety-inducing idea is… whether or not they'll have anxiety at any given moment in time.

3. They come across as a paradoxical mix of outgoing but introverted, very social but rarely out. It is not that they are anti-social, just that they can only take being around others incrementally (which is mostly normal). Yet, on the surface, this may come across as confusing.

4. They make situations worse by trying to suppress their feelings about them. They are extremely uncomfortable with other people seeing them in pain, and they don't want to feel pitied or as though they are compromising anyone's time. Yet, they make things worse for themselves by suppressing, as it actually funnels a ton of energy into making the problem larger and more present than it already was.

5. They are often hyper-aware and highly intuitive. Anxiousness is an evolutionary function that essentially keeps us alive by making us aware of our surroundings and other people's motives. It's only uncomfortable when we don't know how to manage it effectively—the positive side is that it makes you hyper-conscious of what's going on around you.

6. Their deepest triggers are usually social situations. It's not that they feel anxious in an airplane, it's that they feel anxious in an airplane and are stuck around 50 other people. It's not that they will fail a test, but that they will fail a test and everyone in school will find out and think they are incompetent and their parents will be disappointed. It's not that they will lose love, but that they will lose love and nobody will ever love them again.

7. It is not always just a "panicked feeling" they have to hide. It can also be a tendency to worry, catastrophizing, etc. The battle is often (always?) between competing thoughts in their minds.

8. They are deep thinkers and great problem-solvers. One of the benefits of anxiety is that it leads you to consider every worst case scenario, and then subsequently, how to handle or respond to each.

9. They are almost always "self-regulating" their thoughts. They're talking themselves in, out, around, up or down from something or another very often, and increasingly so in public places.

10. They don't trust easily, but they will convince you that they do. They want to make the people around them feel loved and accepted as it eases their anxiety in a way.

11. They tend to desire control in other areas of their lives. They're over-workers or are manically particular about how they dress or can't really seem to let go of relationships if it wasn't their idea to end them.

12. They have all-or-nothing personalities, which is what creates the anxiety. Despite being so extreme, they are highly indecisive. They try to "figure out" whether or not something is right before they actually try to do it.

13. They assume they are disliked. While this is often stressful, it often keeps them humble and grounded at the same time.

14. They are very driven (they care about the outcome of things). They are in equal proportions as in control of their lives as they feel out of control of their lives—this is because they so frequently try to compensate for fear of the unknown.

15. They are very smart but doubt it. A high intelligence is linked to increased anxiety (and being doubtful of one's mental capacity are linked to both).

9

13 Things You're Sick And Tired Of Doing Because Of Your Anxiety

Jane Drinkard

Anxiety has many different faces. Everyone experiences anxiety in their own way. For some of us, it takes a huge, tragic event to get that gut-wrenching, 'want to fall to your knees' sort of feeling and for some of us, it takes a lot less. Yet, in a time where Snapchat, Instagram, Facebook and Twitter are constantly throwing all of your friend's and celebrity's perfectly toned bodies and puppies in your face 24 hours a day, where rail thin is 'good,' AK-47s can be easily bought in a Walmart, systemic racism is rampant and your boyfriend may have just dumped you, it's normal to feel slightly on edge, a little nervous or like you're having a full-fledged panic attack. As someone who has experienced acute anxiety in my life and still does, here are some things I assume you (fellow anxiety sufferers) are fucking done with dealing with:

1. Pretending like you're calm and collected.

The feeling of actually sitting still and feeling at ease is as foreign to you as the concept of understanding the stock market. Most of the time when you're out with friends or at a job interview your very bones feel like they're shaking. To keep a calm exterior requires way more energy than you stored from the two bites of oatmeal you were able to keep down this morning.

2. Hiding your sweaty palms in your sweater.

If you're anything like me, your palms get very sweaty easily. This poses a problem when meeting new people or even texting on your phone. You might prefer sweaters with long sleeves that allow you to 'turtle' your hands in when your hands are feeling extra clammy.

3. Dissecting every little comment until your head starts to spin.

Logically you know your boyfriend didn't intend to call you fat and that he doesn't think that but what did he really mean when he said you looked "healthy and beautiful." The other day he said Becca looked "skinny" but he didn't refer to you that way… so he must think you're fat. He's must not be attracted to you anymore… Your brain competes with you in a mental Olympics to twist every comment or thought into something negative or problematic. Your thoughts coil inwards and inwards until what you're really left with is how you feel about yourself.

4. Calming yourself down only to have your heart speed up again.

Over the years of dealing with these toxic thoughts, you've come up with coping mechanisms to soothe the blow they inflict on your psyche. You breathe deeply. You tell yourself good thoughts. You finally reach a place of semi-zen when your body begins to physically react again. Your heart starts hammering away at your chest, throwing itself against your ribcage, reminding you that no, no you can't relax yet.

5. Being told to "Chill" or "Relax."

There's nothing worse than a Chet or a Jake telling you to "relax" when your body has sent you reeling into panic mode. Because you are smart, you are intelligent, you are only human and you how ridiculous you are being. You are aware that it doesn't really matter but it's the unrest in your chest that won't just shut the fuck up—you wish Chet would just understand that.

6. Adversely being told, "Really? You don't seem anxious."

This response is problematic as well because it's also invalidating. You probably don't 'seem' anxious because of years of working on your outer shell, like a developed callous, and although it makes you slightly happy that you don't come off like a total mess all of the time, you do want people to understand that you're struggling.

7. Rushing to the bathroom solely to have some time to breathe—alone.

Sometimes you just wish your thoughts wouldn't flair up and your chest wouldn't turn into its familiar jackhammer and you could just be; exist and enjoy the crowd. But you can't, and you seem to consistently find yourself staring at your reflection under the florescent lights and wishing you could just stay there forever.

8. Getting lost in your own tangled thoughts.

Your thoughts travel in a patterned web that you can't even really comprehend. You can lose hours following a thread of thoughts that lead you around in aimless circles. Did you make a fool out of yourself? Are you overreacting? Did Allie mean it when she said your joke was lame earlier? Are you pursuing the right career? Are you a good person? Should you just break-up with him? Are you just thinking that because you think that's what he really wants? What do you want for dinner? Are you going to have time to make that? It's exhausting.

9. Constantly feeling annoyed with people when you're really just annoyed with yourself.

This consequence of anxiety is often the hardest to deal with. Other people's ticks and quirks that you find irksome sometimes just reflect qualms you have with yourself. But how can you actually like yourself when so much of yourself (your anxiety) makes you miserable?

10. Picking at your hair, lips, anything to relieve the stress.

You most likely have a calming, destructive habit that temporarily alleviates some of your anxiety. You pick at your hair, your face, your lips or you bite your nails—something that's distracting, if only for a few minutes. This can be the hardest shit to stop because it's a compulsion.

11. Wondering if this knot-in-chest feeling will ever end.

Looking towards the future with anxiety can be extremely exhausting. Mainly because dealing with it today is already tiring enough, you don't want to think about a future with this monster. It's like being in a bad relationship you can't seem to extract yourself from. So you choose to take it day by day.

12. Not being able to fall asleep.

Anxious people and insomniacs are often one in the same. Like a lion stalking its prey, at night, when you're tucked under your shirts and finally completely alone is prime time for your anxiety to strike. You dread the nightly struggle checking your phone to see the hours pass until it's already morning and you have to start all over again.

13. Picking fights with people you love the most

because you need to let your bad mood out somewhere.

You project your insecurities and emotions towards the people that you know will always be there for you unconditionally. They can handle it and are probably used to it, but that doesn't mean you're not sick of treating them like the angels that they are. It's just that sometimes at the end of the day the anxiety machine is programmed to let those feelings out somehow and your family and friends are the first targets. These are the only people capable of punching your anxiety in the face right back, so keep them close and appreciate them.

10

11 Signs You Might Have What's Known As 'High-Functioning' Anxiety

Kendra Syrdal

1. You're constantly called "type A" or "anal retentive" or just "a perfectionist."

People credit you with going above and beyond the call of duty, and always executing things to an nth degree. They poke fun at how you (sometimes unintentionally) seem like you have a "my way or the highway" mentality, like it's just a personality quirk. In reality, the idea of not finishing something or doing something exactly how you've envisioned makes you sick to your stomach. Things like someone coming over and seeing your laundry or missing a deadline by even an hour makes your head spin. They shouldn't seem like a big deal to you, they should be something you can move on from and not dwell on, but they aren't. You obsess and overthink, dwell and stew. So your perfectionist ways (seem) to manage that.

2. You have little ticks that manifest physically, but they just seem like "bad habits" to the outside eye.

Nail biting, hair picking, knuckle cracking, lip chewing. Even picking at your skin or scabs or leaving your cuticles in a bloody mess. They're all little symptoms of your anxiety. You try to keep your panics and nervousness internalized as best you can, but it slips out in these seemingly little things.

3. You don't know when to say when.

"No," is your most underused work in the English language. You don't know how to stay away from reaching your limit. So you pile things on top of each other, always assuming that you can just handle anything and everything. You stretch yourself way too thin and then even after you're breaking, still try to take on more.

4. You can relate to the idea of "compartmentalizing" your emotions.

No one would ever be able to say that you're someone who wears their heart on their sleeve. In fact, you do pretty much the opposite. You're so used to and trained to behave like everything's "fine" even when that couldn't be further from the truth, that you're nearly impossible to read. You've told yourself so many times that you're just being "dramatic" or that no one would understand that you've become a professional level faker of being fine. You rarely let how you're actually feeling show; instead, you just bottle it up and cover it up and hope that it goes away.

5. And because of this, you've been called "stoic" or "unemotional" even when that couldn't be farther from reality.

You've likely gotten a reputation for being rational and logical to a fault because you don't let how you're actually feeling show. Your compartmentalization is next level. Rather than feel your feelings and process them in real time, you put them on a metaphorical shelf in your mind in order to "deal with it later." Problem is, later rarely comes. And then there are all of these anxieties and issues and feelings that pile up on top of each other and it becomes unbearable to manage.

6. You joke about having FOMO—but it's much bigger than that.

It's not so much an "I wish I was included" notion, it's more a deep-seeded fear of missing out on an opportunity. It's the fear of being a bad friend if you don't go somewhere with someone. It's the fear of not being *enough* if, for some reason, you're not able to do everything.

7. You worry about opening up because you'll be accused of "not getting it" because you seemingly live a normal day-to-day life.

There's this idea in your head that because you're still "functioning" your anxiety isn't a problem, and won't be perceived as one. Even if you don't mean to, thinking this way plays into that "trauma Olympics" mentality. It's the idea that because you DON'T do something that's associated with anxiety, or because your anxiety is different in any other way, you don't "qualify." So, rather than say, "This is what I'm struggling with," and open up, you say nothing at all.

8. You lose a lot of sleep.

You keep yourself up at night often. Whether it's because your mind is going 10,000 miles a minute or because you're convinced you can just finish *one more thing*, you're way too familiar with being exhausted. "I'll sleep when I'm dead!" you probably laugh after another sleepless night. But reality? It weighs on you. Both physically, mentally, emotionally. It's a problem.

9. Most people would just call you an "overachiever."

Because when you look at someone who's so good at compartmentalizing, repressing, deflecting, and who's anxiety manifests in a way that makes them hyper-vigilant about very specific things (ie: work, staying occupied, cleaning, list making) it can be so, so easy to only see their successes. But what you don't see, is the battle that it took to GET there. People only see the achievement part, not the stress, the anxiety, the sleeplessness, and the self-deprecation that it took to get there.

10. You joke about needing to be busy to be happy.

"I LOVE being busy."
"I'm happier with a full to-do list."
"Keeping busy keeps me out of trouble!"

It sounds like a glorification of being busy, but really, it's a cover-up for a fear of what will happen if you stop. The *go go go* becomes like a drug. The "always having something do" keeps your mind off of, well, your mind. The constantly chasing something else and doing something is ultimately a big distraction from the anxiety that is ever present in your life.

11. One of your biggest fears is letting people down.

"You could've been better."
"Why did you do this?"
"You're such a bad daughter."
"I wish you were a better friend."

Are those things being said? Probably not. But in your head, in your anxiety-riddled brain, you hear them when presented with the possibility of not doing something at a top tier level. The pressure you put on yourself is *enormous*. And it ultimately stems from the idea that if you don't hold yourself to some near-unachievable standard, you'll be letting someone down. And that breaks your heart. It may be the anxiety talking, but that doesn't mean you don't feel it every single day.

11

23 People On The One Huge Anxiety They Never Tell Anyone About

Maya Kachroo-Levine

1. Really loud music drives me up a wall. I sometimes have to go home early if the bar we are at is too crowded. I lived in Manhattan for a year and was constantly panicking. I had to move to Queens because I needed it to be quiet enough that I could sleep without hyperventilating.

—John, 33

2. Actually, darkness makes me really anxious, and so does really bright light. Sometimes I'll feel overwhelmed with anxiety and won't really understand what brought it on. When that happens, it's typically because I subconsciously reacted to the fact that a room was too dim, or like, headache-inducingly bright.

—Kara, 26

3. Choking. I'm deathly afraid of choking. I have to have water with every meal, and I have to sit it right next to me when I go to bed. No one has ever asked about it, so I've never told anyone.

—Janie, 22

4. For me, sirens really bother me. When I was young, I was taken to the hospital a lot for a year straight because of some health risks (that, thank goodness, they figured out). But when I hear a siren, I still feel that panic, like I have no idea what is about to happen. It's awful, and it happens a lot.

—Karen, 24

5. PLANES. I'm an incredibly anxious flyer, but most relaxants (like Xanax), I'm too scared to even take. Just like when I was at college, I was too scared to smoke, because I'm scared it'll make me more anxious. I know that's irrational, but that's kind of why I don't tell anyone. Telling people you're scared of flying is infuriating because they just start spewing statistics about how you're being ridiculous.

—Elliot, 25

6. I can't get manicures because I'm terrified of nail files. I think it's pretty clear why I don't want to tell people.

—Emma, 22

7. I am very scared of the dark, even in my late 20s. I'm not exactly sure why, but even when my family moved to a country home as a kid for a year, I was so uncomfortable about the fact that it was so dark outside my window at night. For me, moving to a big city actually helped, because there are always lights on somewhere if you're in the heart of the city.

—Aya, 29

8. This might sound morbid, but I have a lot of fears about dying. When I hear about death, it really upsets me, and I'll go through patterns where hearing other people's bad news throws me off for an entire day or two.

—Lindsey, 30

9. Rats, rodents, all tiny animals. Someone once saw a mouse in my apartment, and I had to sleep somewhere else for two weeks and made up an excuse to my roommates.

—Julianne, 24

10. I'm emetophobic, which means I'm really scared of vomiting. I haven't thrown up since I was about 10 years old. It's the reason I don't drink very much, but I've never told anyone.

—Heather, 26

11. I tend to visualize really bad scenarios and then can't get them out of my head. It's actually a big problem because it really affects me and makes me so much less present because I'm often wrapped up in my own upsetting but irrational thoughts.

—Alexa, 24

12. I'm anxious about irrational events. Like, I'm not the type of person who gets anxious because they have a bad boss who makes them feel panicky. No, I'm the one who has severe anxiety about like, getting in a car accident even though I don't drive, being in a plane crash, getting a snake bite. Basically, just things that aren't likely to happen really paralyze me with fear.

—Lilly, 23

13. I get really anxious about the future, but I rarely feel like I can verbalize it. I don't know where I will be in a year—whether my S.O. and I will still be together, if I'll still have a job, what I would do if I didn't.

—Mike, 25

14. Tires screeching. It messes with my head and makes me jump out of my skin.

—Lorraine, 46

15. I have a lot of appearance-related anxieties. I get really stressed about how my skin looks on a certain day, or if I think my hair is frizzing out when I'm out at a bar, I'll leave. I don't tell people because they just think it sounds so trivial, and I don't want to hear it.

—Roxanne, 29

16. I've noticed I'm really anxious about one-on-one time with anyone. People assume I'm social because I can do group settings pretty much anytime, but if I'm just with one other person, I just feel like I'm in the hot sea. It's been a problem for me while trying to date, and even while trying to just keep close friends.

—Johanna, 22

17. Not loud noises, but sharp or screeching noises make me so anxious. If I hear tires squeal, I'm a nervous wreck for the next few hours.

—Kelsey, 37

18. I can't help but be super anxious about what other people think. I'll meet someone and be over analyzing something I said to them five days later.

—Jake, 24

19. I have separation anxiety, so when I am far away from family or my boyfriend, I'll be really nervous about their whereabouts, and I can tell they get sick of my constant phone calls, but we haven't really talked about the root cause of why I get so anxious.

—Mary, 25

20. Nothing makes me more anxious on an airplane than a crying baby.

—Eric, 28

21. I have a really hard time with my anxiety when everyone around me is sick because I'm a bit of a hypochondriac. On the one hand, I don't want to show people how freaked out I am that they'll make me sick, but I also sometimes can't help it.

—Kayla, 32

22. I have a lot of relationship anxiety because I don't know where we are going to be staying together or not. And that's not an anxiety you want to bring up, but it's also one that really sticks with you, and that I've been really struggling with for about six months.

—Tania, 27

23. Natural disasters. I live in California, and as a transplant, I have constant panic attacks about earthquakes.

—JC, 20

12

Newsflash: Telling People With Anxiety To 'Just Relax' Doesn't Work

Ari Eastman

Anywhere you go, you're bound to run into someone who stands ready with terrible advice.

cough (browse through my archive for proof!) *cough*

People mean well. Like that one girl on Facebook who SWEARS denim maxi skirts look good. Or when your friend once suggested eating a Beefy Crunchy Burrito from Taco Bell before you went out on a first date.

Yikes.

I think we're all full of bullshit.

At least somewhat. Me, you, your best friend, the teacher you idolized. Even the wisest person in the world has advised someone poorly. At least once.

And I don't even think that's necessarily a bad thing. People try. They advise to the best of their ability. We're human, so we're going to be flawed, and flawed with how we try to problem solve.

But by far, one of the topics people seem to give THE WORST advice on is good ole anxiety.

Ah, anxiety! My childhood pal. The thing that's kept me (unasked for) company longer than anything else I can remember. It's sweet, really. Anxiety never wants me to feel alone, always wants to remind me they're around. So generous of you, anxiety!! My longest and most committed relationship. Here's looking at you, A.

For some reason, everyone thinks they're an expert on anxiety. Apparently, Tumblr gives out doctorate degrees. Who knew?

Does everyone experience anxious moments? You bet. Does everyone suffer from chronic anxiety? Nope. They're two different beasts, my friend.

Anxiety feels like having all your senses heightened, but not in any cool Superhero way.

You're panicked about irrational things. You overthink even the most mundane and simple tasks. Your mind is plagued with worst case scenarios, and it feels like you're powerless to stop it.

Do I know the best way to combat anxiety? Nope. I learn what works for me, but even that's always changing. But what I do know? Telling someone to "relax" is not relaxing.

When you tell someone to relax, you aren't being helpful. You're just robbing them of validity. You're telling them, "This thing you have isn't real. Just stop it." You're denying their experience, their struggle.

If people could just *relax*, don't you think they'd be doing it?

Like seriously tell me, do you think you're the first person to suggest it? OH, THANK GOD! WE HAVE UNLOCKED THE SECRET. WE HAVE FOUND THE CURE!!

When you tell someone to relax, you're stressing them out even more. Because now not only do they have the initial anxiety, now they feel like a failure for not being able to relax. Now they have two things to make them feel shitty.

And that's just not helping anybody.

I don't think people mean to make things worse. Like I said, we all do it. We all have our narcissistic moments where we think we're Gurus and our words are obviously Brilliant and The Answer To Everything.

But when it comes to anxiety, there are far better things you can say to someone than "relax." Seriously.

So here's a thought—maybe next time, just don't?

13

The Most Important Thing You Need To Remember When Your Anxiety Sets In

Kim Quindlen

I don't think anxiety ever goes away. At least, for me it doesn't. Maybe there are some #blessed people out there who have figured out a magical way to defeat their anxiety once and for all. But for most of us, there's no cure. There's no mountain you climb, or bridge you cross so that you can get to the other side where you'll be free from worry and fear. It's more about learning to deal with anxiety when it comes and learning to treasure those beautiful moments in time where it's temporarily absent.

A life plagued by anxiety is one of racing heartbeats and fast breathing. Your shoulders often feel heavy and sometimes you're almost sure that you can see a dark cloud hanging over you. There's a strange fear that doesn't seem to stem from anything specific. It's just *fear*. It's just *there*.

Sometimes you can't enjoy a nice, peaceful train ride. Or a trip to the movies with your friends. Because the minute you sit down, you're forced to be with your own thoughts. They start running around in all different directions. You're thinking of possible dangerous scenarios or things that have caused you anxiety in the past. Or you just feel scared for no reason at all. It just happens, and you wish it wouldn't.

It's worse in the winter. So much worse. The days are short and the weather is cold. It seems like it's *always* dark. The small amount of sunlight we experience during the day doesn't even feel like sunlight. It just feels like a strange and brief phase of the day that will be over quickly. Darkness will descend in no time.

This is when it's the hardest. When everyone feels cold and bitter and cranky and cooped up. We can't distract ourselves with light breezes and bright colors. We can't walk around outside for hours and free ourselves from our own heads. It's winter. Everything is dead and gray and muted and cold. This is when your state of mind and your way of thinking can either make you or break you.

You have to acknowledge that you probably will not defeat anxiety. You don't need to focus all of your energy on "fixing yourself" or finding a cure. Stop making yourself feel like there's something wrong with you. Stop making yourself feel ashamed of your anxiety. Stop being frustrated with yourself. Just because you can't beat anxiety doesn't mean you're letting it win.

Yes, you're probably going to have to deal with it for the rest of your life. Not all the time, of course. Sometimes you will have incredibly wonderful periods of time where you don't have any anxiety. You can go days without it. You can go months without it. Sometimes you will go years before you have to deal with it again. But often, regardless of how long it's been, anxiety will find its way back to you. You do not have control over the cure, but the beautiful part is that you do have control over how you handle it.

The most important thing you have to work on is your state of mind. When anxiety starts to take over, it's tempting to give in to your thoughts. To let yourself crumble under the fear and the worry and the terror. What you have to remember is that you're not alone. You are not by yourself. You may feel like you are the only person in the world to ever feel like a prisoner inside their own mind, but you are not. There are so many others who have been where you've been, but they eventually got free. Not free from anxiety, necessarily, but free from the dark way of thinking that anxiety can cause.

A lot of people struggle with anxiety. Not everyone, but enough people to show you that there are others who have gotten through this, just like you will. You're struggling now. You're terrified now. You feel alone now. You're telling yourself it will be okay. You're telling yourself you will get through this. You're telling yourself you will be stronger when you come out on the other side. But you have a hard time believing it. That's okay. As long as you're trying to believe it, as long as you are wanting to believe it, those thoughts will carry you through the darker moments. And eventually, they will start to make sense. They will start to seem *possibly* true.

A lot of people will give you a lot of different advice on how to deal with anxiety. Some of it will work for you, and some of it won't. Some of the things that do work for you will not work for your friend or your coworker. Everyone is different. Everyone's mind is different. So everyone will deal with anxiety a different way.

Here's what you need to remember: there's a lot of advice floating out there about dealing with anxiety because *so many people* have had to deal with it. So when you're feeling ashamed or frustrated or exhausted or embarrassed about your anxiety, just remind yourself that you are normal. You are not a freak. You are not the only person in the world that has ever been this terrified. A lot of us are fighting it. A lot of us are scared. A lot of us have had bad nights that we didn't think were ever going to end, just like you have.

You are human. Which means you will get through it, just like so many other people have. You will not defeat it forever. But you will learn how to be okay—and more importantly, how to be *happy*—in spite of it.

14

26 Completely Ridiculous Things You Stress About When You Suffer From Anxiety

Holly Riordan

1. Hanging out with one of your close friends that you should be completely comfortable around. But for some reason, you're still worried you'll run out of things to talk about and bore them to death.

2. Walking up to a register to pay. And then struggling to shove your change in your wallet before the people in line behind you get fed up.

3. Being too quiet during a group conversation. You don't want everyone to think you're a snob, but you just can't think of anything to say.

4. Showing up too early. If you're the first person there, you'll start to worry if you showed up at the wrong place or on the wrong day.

5. Waiting for someone to text you back. If it takes them a little too long to answer, then you'll worry that you've been annoying them.

6. Standing in line. The entire time, you're practicing what you're going to say once you reach the end of that line.

7. Finding a seat on a crowded bus or train. And being forced to sit next to a complete stranger on a crowded bus or train.

8. Hearing a notification on your phone after you sent out a semi-risky email.

9. Driving by a cop or walking through a metal detector, even though you didn't do anything wrong at all.

10. Sitting in the middle of a row at the movie theater, where you'll have to scoot past strangers to get to the bathroom.

11. Trying to figure out if the single stalled bathroom already has someone in it. You'd die of embarrassment if you accidentally walked in on someone else.

12. Telling a joke that bombs. Sometimes, you won't even test out your jokes, because you're too worried about looking silly.

13. Forgetting something important. Before you leave for a concert, you'll check your bag twenty times to make sure you remembered the tickets.

14. Picking clothes for a party. You don't want to be the fanciest person in the room. But you don't want to be the only one in jeans, either.

15. Entering a packed classroom after everyone else has already sat down.

16. Making a turn onto a super busy highway. You're terrified of cutting someone off or crashing.

17. Asking a complete stranger for directions. You hate initiating conversations.

18. Getting your credit card declined. You know you always pay your bills on time, but *still*. You hate paying with a card.

19. Eating in front of other people. You don't want to finish faster than them and look like a slob. But you don't want to hold them up by taking too long to eat. And you don't want to get sauce all over your face.

20. Calling up your dentist or gyno to make an appointment. Or, really, calling anyone.

21. Ordering at Chipotle. There are just too many questions to answer.

22. Posting on Facebook or Instagram and not getting any "likes." Honestly, when that happens, you go back and delete the post entirely.

23. Going on first dates. What do you wear? How do you act? What do you say? You're swarmed by questions.

24. Being called into your boss' office. You're praying you didn't do anything to get yourself fired.

25. Leaving the house. It doesn't matter where you're going. You feel the safest in your own room.

26. Thinking about all of the ways that you could make a complete and utter fool of yourself throughout the day.

15

My Anxiety Isn't 'Quirky'—It's Exhausting

Elizabeth Weinberger

It's a Friday night and all of your friends are over at your place eating dollar-store tortilla chips and microwaveable cheese dip when all of a sudden Johnny throws up in the middle of the room! *Come on, duuuuuuude!!*

Maybe it was the marked-down cheese dip that got to him (my bad), or maybe it was the beefy burrito he scarfed down from Taco Bell on the way over... either way, the smell coming from that gigantic heap of Johnny's stomach acid instantly makes everyone start throwing up too.

So now, it's this huge big barf-tastrophy: a barf-ocolypse of sorts.

In other words, it's a big disgusting heap of throw-up which continues to grow, the smell of barf making your group of friends continuously empty their stomachs onto the already cringe-worthy apartment floor.

Not a pretty picture, is it?

Well, that's what anxiety feels like: a group of friends constantly throwing up in your head. Every thought, every plan, and every "what if?" compiled, constructing this huge shitshow freakout you can't stop.

I have so much anxiety that *my anxiety has anxiety.* It's like trying to maneuver through 879 tabs in a browser while also attempting to have a meaningful conversation with a friend and simultaneously trying to study for a test.

It's crazy. It's chaotic. And it never stops.

People who don't have anxiety don't fully understand it. I've had people tell me, "Don't worry about it! We will get it done tomorrow." Or, "It's okay! If it's meant to work out, it will work out."

And I just want to say right back to them, "No, it's not okay." And, "I WILL worry about it, thank you very much."

This is just how my weird brain works.

I have two planners in my purse just so that I can try and keep everything organized. I'm constantly making lists in the notepad on my phone in order to not forget anything. Whenever I have to participate in a group project at school I end up taking the reins because I'm too afraid everyone else will wait till the last minute and it won't get done.

I have to control everything or my anxiety worsens.

My mind is insane.

Sometimes these "quirks" work to my benefit, but the majority of the time this craziness doctors call anxiety is extremely debilitating.

Anxiety IS a mental health disorder. Some people think that people who suffer from anxiety can just change their mindset. They think it's not so much a mental disorder as it is some kind of need to control everything. But that is not the case.

It plagues my mind. It makes me think of the worst case scenario all the time; it makes me worry about anything and everything, and it frequently takes over my life. It dictates almost everything I do.

The group of friends throwing up in my brain does not stop. Ever.

Sometimes I can put a TV on in that vomit-filled apartment and drown out the noises—pretend it's not happening for a bit—but then it returns.

I'm tired of people telling me it's "easy" to think differently. It's not. I'm tired of people telling me to "stop thinking negatively" and to "just let it go" and "stop trying to control everything" because I can't.

People need to understand that anxiety is a mental health disorder, and it can't just be turned off. It's so common that 3 million people are diagnosed a year! Three million people who cannot function normally because of the thoughts in their heads. Three million people who have a barf-ocolypse occurring in their heads.

If you had a group of friends throwing up in your head constantly, I don't think you'd want other people to telling you "don't worry" about it either.

16

This Is How Anxiety Takes Over Your Life (And This Is How You Take It Back)

Lauren Jarvis-Gibson

My first job out of college was stressful to say the least. I would make small mistakes and get yelled at almost immediately, and without real explanation. I would perform to the best of my abilities and still be insulted or ridiculed. My best was not good enough. My 150% effort was irrelevant in other people's eyes.

I didn't have to do this. But, I thought that if I did this, then people would appreciate the effort.

So, I started coming to work by 7:30 AM. I would clean the offices, wipe down the whiteboards, empty the dishwashers, and make sure the copiers were on. I would run from kitchen to kitchen, stocking up the coffee to make sure each flavor was full. I would sprint down the halls to make sure everyone had the correct newspapers and would be in a full sweat by 8:30 AM.

I didn't have to do this. I didn't have to run around the office building like I was training for a marathon. But, I thought that if I did this, then people would appreciate the effort. And maybe then, I would feel more at ease. Maybe then, I would feel more comfortable in a place I had to spend eight hours of my day at.

And it kicked me in the ass. Hard. Combined with the pressure I had put on myself, mixed with the stress of this job's work environment, I crumbled.

I did everything outside of my job description just to please people, just to get a simple "thank you" or even a nod of encouragement. I did everything in my power to do as much as I could in a day, to feel some sort of release afterward. But, instead of feeling good about myself at the end of the day, my anxiety came back in full force.

And it kicked me in the ass. Hard. Combined with the pressure I had put on myself, mixed with the stress of this job's work environment, I crumbled. It happened on a Wednesday. I remember not being particularly stressed out that day and everything seemed to be going fine. Then, around 2:30, I felt my hands and feet go numb. I was knocked down by a burning in my chest that felt like a match was lit right at my heart. I remember my body feeling like it was going to turn to dust any minute. I called my mom in tears, and she drove me to the ER.

I didn't know what was wrong with me. I had experienced panic attacks before, but they never were as severe as this one. I thought that this had to be a stroke and I remember people in the ER looking so calm and collected. But, my insides were on fire and I wanted to shout out, "I'm dying, can't you see that?" Finally, the nurse did an EKG on me and other typical tests you see them do on *Grey's Anatomy*. When she got the results back, she looked at me and told me—"You're fine."

I learned that I was not Hercules, but I was a human being who had limits. And that was okay.

But I wasn't fine. And I'm still not fine. How can someone who has a panic attack for three hours straight be okay afterward? I had run from my anxiety for ten months, and it had finally caught me red handed. I had hit a dead end, but also began a new chapter in my life. I learned that I was not Hercules, but I was a human being who had limits. And that was okay.

I'm learning and realizing that sometimes, we all need to slow down. To take a breath. To walk instead of run. It's okay to not be the best at our job. It's okay to leave a job that you find is causing you harm. It's okay to pause when you need to pause. Ask yourself if what you are doing is benefitting you, and if it's not, then stop. Please talk to someone and don't keep your demons to yourself, because it will only make them stronger.

This world can be a scary place full of uncertainty and of pain. And if we all keep sprinting and rushing to the finish line, we are going to burn out. We need to take every day to be kind to ourselves and to press pause on our lives for a moment. Take a second to gather all your negative thoughts that are trying to spill out of your brain, and let it out. And then let it go. It's okay to crumble once in a while, but it's not okay to ignore what your body and your brain are trying to tell you. So, don't brush it off. Listen.

17

What It Feels Like When You Let Your Anxiety Take Over Your Life

Sarah R. Hughes

Anxiety is strange, mostly because when you finally realize you have it you realize it is like a piece of furniture you have always been around, something you have gotten used to, but something you have always wanted to move to the other side of the room. **You don't know when it got there, or even how sometimes, but it is the ugliest chair you've ever seen, and you're sure even if you put a "FREE" sign on it at the end of your driveway, it would sit there for years, haunting you from its new spot beside the mailbox too.**

Looking back, I guess I was always a little anxious. I was always looking over my shoulder for the nameless and the faceless. I had unshakable fears and worried about things that would never happen for as long as I can remember which is as early as three.

I began fighting the battle nobody knows about before I even knew about it. It sounds like the plot

for some empowering dramedy starring Zooey Kazan, but in fact, all it has done is left me weak and beaten.

I remember when I was young I wondered why I felt so sad and scared most of the time. I wondered why I feared things that hadn't happened and why I took precautions for things that would never happen. As I gathered a flashlight, batteries, a water bottle, and a can of chicken noodle soup to hide under my bed, I knew I was insane.

I was only seven, living in the Rocky Mountains. Tornadoes could not touch down there, but I knew I would be the one to get sucked up into one never to be heard from again. Crazy or not, I stashed my survival kit under my bed until my mother found it and gingerly placed these things back where I had found them without saying anything. Later I learned she had been anxious for a long time too.

As I grew, the ugly chair that was my anxiety faded in and out of my life. I white-knuckled adolescence like an ice road trucker praying for a warming beam of sun. All the while I still wondered where is this feeling coming from? What am I bracing for?

I didn't have cancer or MS. Nobody in my immediately family was dead. We had experienced hardships, but nothing my friends had not experienced.

Why was I like this?

And I supposed that was the thing that made me most anxious and still makes me most anxious. I don't even know why I feel anxious. Nothing will happen. **There will be no reason for anything to happen. I, however, will find some reason to believe the worst.**

There are some days when I see the chair clearly, it is in the middle of the room, and I am too exhausted to ignore it. With its offensive upholstery and third-rate stitching, I collapse into it. I don't want to and I hate myself for it, but who can fight all the time I think as I attempt to console myself and try desperately not to become anxious over allowing myself to feel anxious.

I am ashamed to admit that sometimes just giving in feels good.

Fighting is so hard. It takes all of your energy to keep out the dark that there is no energy to enjoy the light. What other choice do some of us have but to light a candle in our darkness? To revel in it a little in order to have at least a few moments of peace in the day before we are a crying mess on the bathroom floor just like the next person?

I do not enjoy my anxiety. It is a piece of furniture that was gifted to me. Sometimes I feel guilty for thinking about getting rid of it, but it is likely that is the anxiety talking to. One day I will look up and I will know I have beaten it. It will be gone. **Until then, some days I sit, igniting a candle in my own darkness just to have some light.**

18

Read This If Social Anxiety Really Fucks With Your Dating Life And It Sucks

Jacob Geers

Last week I was talking to a guy who I'm not talking to anymore, and from the very moment we started texting back and forth, my life suddenly became so much more stressful. And not like butterflies in the stomach nervousness, but totally all-consuming stress and pressure. I couldn't focus at work because I was just on edge with when he would text me, and what he would text me, and what I would text back, and, and, and…

Whenever I start talking to someone new I feel suffocated in a cocoon of commitment, fear, and anxiety. I am not someone who can just go with the flow. I am not someone who can just passively wait for what happens next. I am not someone who can date (probably).

I stress every step of the way. I stress about talking to someone. I stress about talking to them too much. I stress about not talking to them enough. I worry about every joke I try to make and every sign of affection I try to initiate.

Sometimes I honestly think that my social anxiety will prevent me from ever finding a happy relationship. I will never be able to "put myself out there"—I don't socialize well. I'm not a good flirt. I'm not good at fusing together casual small-talk with subtle stories about how great I am. I'm even less good at going out and throwing caution to the wind. While my fellow partygoers are helping themselves to Long Island after Long Island, I am wondering how late I have to stay before it's socially acceptable to go home.

And so my friends have loving partners that they spend their time with, and I eat, sleep, and live alone. And I'm not miserable for it, but I can't help but feel a tiny bit of emptiness inside of me. **And I can't help but feel just a little, teeny, tiny bit bitter about this pervasive anxiety.**

I can't help but feel like I'm spinning my wheels.

I want to be able to give someone a chance. I want to be able to not worry about tomorrow, and just enjoy today. I want to date someone long enough to actually see if they might be good for me. **I want to be able to do these things, but I can't.** There are those, like my well-meaning friends, that might rebut, "Oh, it might be hard but you just have to do it." But these people don't know what it's like to feel physically ill after trying to hold a conversation with some cute boy on the dance floor. They don't understand. How could they? People equate social anxiety disorder with just feeling anxious from time to time, when the two are almost as different as could be.

And I guess, for those of us with social anxiety, we just plod on. We just do our best. We just try to manage our problem and move forward the best we can. **As much as it sucks, I truly believe that our anxiety might just be filtering out the people who wouldn't be good for us anyway. If what someone values in me is my ability to dance and have superficial conversation at the bar, we probably aren't a good fit anyway.**

And I know, it's much easier to type those words out than it is to sit alone while all our friends have someone stumbled into someone.

But we should take heart. We should dare to believe in ourselves, and dare to believe in the happy ending we deserve. After all, that is the first step to conquering social anxiety.

19

10 Reasons Why People With Anxiety Have Such A Hard Time Finding Love

Lauren Jarvis-Gibson

1. They over criticize themselves.

They truly believe that they aren't good enough for the person they are dating and are over critical of every choice they make. They constantly beat themselves over mistakes and can't get a grasp on their own self-worth.

2. They fear having panic attacks.

They are always tense, anticipating and waiting for a panic attack to begin. Usually, they won't be able to predict when a panic attack could happen, but because of how powerful these attacks can be, they are constantly worried about when it will strike.

3. They view first dates as their personal hell.

They will spend hours trying to give themselves pep talks to have the courage to even go through with a first date. Meeting someone new is absolutely terrifying in the first place, and when you have anxiety, it can be truly petrifying.

4. They won't settle for just anyone.

Not only are they looking for a good boyfriend or girlfriend, but they are looking for someone who will understand their mental illness. They can't date someone who is ignorant to their problem, and they need someone who can give them empathy and support.

5. They feel alone with their anxiety.

When you don't struggle with anxiety, you can't possibly know or understand what it feels like to be plagued with this illness. People with anxiety always feel alone in their own head, and also hate to feel like a burden to others.

6. They struggle talking comfortably with someone new.

Talking with a stranger is extremely difficult to do for someone with anxiety. They worry about not having enough conversation starters and fret about the conversation going downhill. They also want to act like they are calm and collected, which is nearly impossible for them to do.

7. They are consumed with thoughts of the relationship ending.

As soon as they are in a great relationship, they start to become concerned about the ending. They can become consumed with thoughts of their partner leaving them out of the blue, or breaking up with them because they found someone better. They are always worrying about ending up alone once again.

8. They worry their significant other deserves someone better than them.

They hate to be a burden and are usually definite people pleasers. They tend to think that their significant other deserves someone who doesn't have anxiety and that they would be better off without them.

9. They will do absolutely anything to avoid confrontation and arguments.

Individuals with anxiety despise any type of confrontation. While some fights can be healthy, they will do anything and everything in their power to ignore or run away from arguments. This can cause even more tension in their relationships, because they will shut their partner out no matter how their significant other approaches the problem.

10. They can start depending on their partner for anxiety related problems.

They can deal with anxiety on their own. But, when they start to have a wonderful relationship and their partner learns how to comfort them when they are suffering, they worry they might grow dependent on this person. They don't want to become fully dependent on their boyfriend or girlfriend, because if the relationship ends up not working out, they will have to start all over again.

20

What It's Like To Fall In Love When You Have Anxiety

Brianna Wiest

We like to believe in solutions—especially ones that come in the form of other people. We worry about a problem, fix the problem, the worrying goes away, we assume it all happens outside of us... until the worrying comes back. The trouble with assuming the problem is outside is that we always think the answer is, too.

The thing about falling in love when you have anxiety is that feeling happier about one part of your life doesn't mean you're less worried about others. When you intensify your sensitivity to one emotion, you do it across the board. The more you love, the more you fear. Acquiring one great thing in your life doesn't nullify the others. People think that the solution to pain is joy, but it works the other way around; the more receptive you are to happiness, the more receptive you are to everything else.

Falling in love when you have anxiety is all of these things. It begins with the idea that another person will fix it. It follows with the realization that they won't. And then comes the important part, the real work of love. The dismantling.

Falling in love becomes a process of learning that it's okay. You get over your fears about being seen and known and loved, because one day at a time, one step at a time, one challenge at a time, you are. You learn that you can be comfortable naked, or that you can meet their friends and get along. You learn, mostly, that the things you've feared the most were actually things that would bring you so much happiness.

You worry about silly, little things. You overthink conversations and fear how they see the roll of your stomach. You think yourself in and out of situations that have no bearing on reality. You learn that love may not be the answer to anxiety, but it sure as hell is a great companion.

More than anything else, though, you learn there's something much more profound than being loved for being perfect, and that's being loved even when you're not. That's all we're really trying to control with our anxiety anyway. We're just filtering through fears about whether or not there are aspects of us that are undeserving of someone else's affection.

When you fall in love when you have anxiety, you learn that love isn't what happens when it's easy, it's what happens when you choose each other in spite of the fact that it's not.

21

This Is How It Feels To Love Someone With Anxiety

Bhavya Kaushik

People have issues. There is no other way to say it. I know this because I have been fighting with depression for the last six years. I still do it every single night. People fight against their inner demons, which could be anything. Anyone. Just like the flu, anyone can experience anxiety issues. I can't contemplate and say whether it's a good or a bad thing. It is just something that you learn to live with.

You try to act normal and keep your cool every time you are with someone who is experiencing a deeply rooted problem like anxiety. When it comes to love, you always walk an extra mile or meet your partner halfway. If you are dating someone who has anxiety issues, you need to walk more than just an extra mile. You don't meet them halfway. You go all the way to the end of the tunnel. Nevertheless, it is one such thing that you can never regret. I have been in love with someone who has anxiety issues and I won't have it any other way.

1. You won't have an "ideal" relationship.

It won't be like one of those relationships that you read about in YA books. You can't compare it with anything else in the world. It is like falling in love with someone for the first time all over again. You would make an effort to know someone from deep within.

What makes them anxious? What cools them down? What is their go-to movie? What is their favorite cuisine? What is their safe place, their sanctuary? What is their story?

These are the kinds of questions you try to solve in the process of falling in love with them. You don't try to become their soulmate or twin flame. You become their skin and bones.

2. There's a lot of planning and less spontaneity.

Because the thought of leaving everything just like that and going for a romantic weekend getaway would be a nightmare for your partner. From having a movie night to going out for dinner, everything needs to planned (and re-checked). Mark all those crowded places off as well.

3. But you'll share a different level of intimacy.

But that's the thing. If you really love them and wants to have a great time with them, you won't be bothered by their choices. Who would like to go to a concert or a movie theater when you can spend hours with your partner talking about The Big Bang and time-travel?

4. Your love won't be enough at times.

There would always come a time when their anxiety would take over and you would find it hard to calm them down. They would be inconsolable and you would realize that even your love can't be enough to make them feel like home. Give them enough time and space. That's the best thing you can do. Just let them know that you will always be there for them. Always. Because it's either all or nothing.

5. You have to make a constant effort.

Loving someone is not an event. It's a process. Every single morning, you would fall in love with them in a whole new way (which would be an experience in itself). But it's not as dreamy as it sounds. Every day, you need to make an effort to fall in love with them. You would discover something new about them and despite all the odds you would learn to see beyond the obvious.

6. But it's so damn worth it.

Because they would never let you down. They would mean each and every word that would be spoken by them. They would make you believe that storms are mild and innocence in overrated. They would give their heart and soul (and everything in between) to you. They would love you in the most effortless way. You would feel it in your bones.

7. Your relationship is built on honesty and trust.

There is this thing about those who have anxiety issues. They are quite concerned about their future. They can't let their loved ones down. For them, honesty and trust mean everything. They will let you experience a whole new definition of loyalty, which would bring a radical change in you.

8. It's an unforgettable experience.

If you would sail through all the ups and downs, you'll realize how effortlessly you have created a lasting relationship. Being with them might be a task in itself at times, but deep within you would realize that they are just like anyone else. They have their share of insecurities just like every one of us. We all are a little broken and flawed. At least they are true to themselves and are not afraid to show their flaws. This is what makes them so damn special!

No one would be able to see the dynamics involved in your relationship. Only the two of you would realize how far you have come. At the end of the day, loving someone with anxiety issues would be just like loving someone who is flawed and honest. And you know what? It's okay! Aren't we all a little flawed after all? Embrace their flaws and walk all the way down to the end of the tunnel.

Because they are so damn worth it.

22

50 Things A Girl With Anxiety Needs From Her Partner

Kelli Rose

As a woman with anxiety, I can tell you right now, I know that I am not the easiest person to love. Some days are harder than others. Some days I feel as if I am spinning out of control and can't get anything right. I know that I may not be full of sunshine and daisies but I have people that love me very much, even when I can't see it myself. Some people understand it because they've been there; some people think it's a figment of your imagination. Whether it's what you would consider "real" or not, it would mean the world to your anxious loved one if you could take a step back and listen to our needs and apply a few simple actions that would make our world a much easier place to handle. Let's talk about some simple ways to ease your loved one's anxiety, shall we?

1. Please for the love of God do not force us to make plans at the very last minute.

Rest assured, we already have our entire day or week planned out before you come up to us with some last minute dinner plans or an outing to a bar with the girlfriends after so-and-so's latest break-up. It takes a lot for us to get motivated to get out into the world and ready to face other human beings. Please don't make us have to do that before we're mentally prepared. More importantly, don't be offended when we say no.

2. Don't say things like, "Look at me in the eyes."

This is definitely impossible for us most of the time. Let's not make things awkward by me having to openly deny your request for eye contact.

3. Don't take if offensively if we don't want to hold your hand.

Our personal bubble is a sacred place. When someone touches us, it can be a suffocating feeling, even if you're trying to be loving or comforting. It's nothing against you; we will return the love when we are ready.

4. Understand that small talk is excruciating.

I mean, really. Let's not settle for those obligatory comments about the weather, what we've been up to lately or the scores of the latest football game. Get to the point or be quiet. I truly appreciate the silence much more than the unnecessary chatter.

5. We desperately need some time to recharge after being social.

It is emotionally draining to be around a group of people. Once we're finally out of that situation, it feels like we have run a mental marathon. We need some down time with silence, solitude and a few days to recoup before we're ready to face the world again.

6. It's much easier if you will just make plans for us.

Truly, the least amount of options that I feel I am being forced to choose from, the better.

7. "Meeting the parents" never sounds like a fun idea. Let's try to avoid this for as long as possible.

We already hardcore judge ourselves, what we say, how we look, and how we act. We will obsess over whether or not your folks approved of us. Let us become more comfortable, and let us prepare. This is a serious thing, and we want to get it right!

8. Don't volunteer for us to host family members or friends in our home without my consent.

This is definitely something that needs to be discussed beforehand. Our home is our safe place. Don't invite people in to our safe place if we aren't feeling so groovy that day. It makes it so much harder to entertain when we aren't at our best.

9. Help us stay on top of upcoming plans/events and their dates so that we don't stress out as much about having to remember it by ourselves.

We'll obsess over it anyway but it would just be nice if we feel like we aren't the only ones worrying about that sort of thing.

10. Fill up the gas tank before you come home so we don't have to go to the gas station.

People don't realize how extremely anxious gas stations can make people. The entire experience is filled with possible interactions with other people, remembering pump numbers and what you came inside to get, and trying to hurry so the person waiting for your pump doesn't get aggravated and honk the horn. It's really a lot to take in, and none of it is fun.

11. Don't make fun of us if we don't feel like speaking through a drive-thru window.

Speaking to others isn't easy, even if you can't see their faces. This is a real thing.

12. Offer to go inside a store if it isn't necessary that we go in ourselves.

The best way to deal with a potentially awkward situation is to not deal with it at all.

13. Don't send us texts like, "I have a question," or, "We need to talk about something later."

This will drive us literally crazy, and we will beat ourselves up trying to figure it out. Don't do this to ANYONE, for that matter. Ever. It's just wrong.

14. If there is any bill that can't be paid online, then pay it on the phone yourself.

If it's online, then don't worry- we got you! Please don't make us speak to anyone on the phone, though. The horror.

15. Don't leave us home alone when the cable guy or some service person is scheduled to come fix something at our house.

It's already overwhelming knowing that a stranger is scheduled to come to your house. It's even more overwhelming knowing that you'll have to let them in and speak to them.

16. Answer the door if someone is unexpectedly knocking, and we aren't aware of who it could possibly be.

I know it sounds silly, but this is a life saver. When you have to mentally prepare before you socialize with others, unexpected visitors are not your friends.

17. Ask if we would prefer for you to drive when we're going anywhere.

Driving can be a lot to handle, as well. (See more about this topic on Reason #27) If we aren't feeling up to the challenge, then it would be just lovely if you would volunteer to drive instead.

18. Don't call us if whatever you need to say can easily be sent via text message.

"Sorry I didn't answer my phone when you called. That's not what I use it for."

19. If you know that we're out of something, then pick it up at the store on your way home instead of asking us to take a special trip to get it.

A lot can happen to us during the day so you never know how we're feeling until you get there. We could've had a hard day, and facing people doesn't sound so appealing to us. It could end up being the straw that broke the camel's back.

20. Don't make unnecessary noises, ever.

The more noises that we hear, the more scattered our brains become. Please don't add fuel to the fire.

21. Don't touch us for no reason. I mean, no reason.

Once again—personal bubble, my friend. Do not burst my bubble.

22. If we are standing at a store waiting to check out, then take the initiative to speak to the cashier and pay for our items for us, even if we have to hand you the money.

Again, small talk. Awkwardness. Anxiety.

23. Don't put the spotlight on us when we're talking with a group of people by asking us a random question.

We're really trying very hard to be present but blend in with the scenery. Being the center of a conversation is not on the list of things we're trying to accomplish here.

24. Always remember the look we give you when we're in public and are ready to leave.

Just pay attention. You know what look I'm talking about.

25. Take into consideration how long we stay at any given place.

The sooner we can leave, the sooner we can get back to our safe place.

26. Remember that we really don't like surprises, and definitely don't talk about a surprise before you intend to reveal it to us.

This is just as, if not more, excruciating than the dreaded "We have to talk" text messages. If you're going to surprise us with a gift, then just do it. If you're wanting to surprise us with a trip, then run it by us first before you make plans. We will still be thankful for the gesture.

27. Be extremely attentive when you're driving us somewhere.

Please, please, please pay attention to the road and watch where you are going. We aren't in control, and that's a problem for us. Even if you're a good driver, we're still scared as hell about all the possibilities of what could go wrong on this journey. Be aware! That includes no texting and driving!

28. Don't ask us to entertain someone that you're speaking with so that you can go do something else.

This only leads to small talk, and it only drains our soul. Just say no.

29. Don't get aggravated when we ask the same questions over and over again just so we can be sure.

We can never be too sure, and sometimes our insecurities and fears will never silence in our heads. Humor us, if you will, but it makes us feel better.

30. When we think that something is wrong and we want you to go check it out, please be polite and comply, even if you think it's silly or unreasonable.

Even if that means checking to make sure the door is locked after we've already been in bed for over an hour.

31. When we tell you that we're afraid of something, believe us.

Please don't force us to do something that completely terrifies us, even if it seems like a ridiculous fear to you. It is very real and traumatic for us.

32. When we're having a panic attack, please don't speak to us or touch us.

We know that you're just trying to help but believe us, we know how we're supposed to ride this out. Nothing that you say or do is helping. Give us space. Give us silence. Then, give us comfort when we're exhausted from how draining an anxiety attack really is, and don't ask questions about it or draw attention to us until we're ready to talk.

33. Don't try to be love-y if we're not feeling it.

I promise you, we're not trying to be cold or unloving towards you. Sometimes we just need our personal bubble to not be popped. Just because we don't want to cuddle, that doesn't mean that we don't love you very much.

34. Never be afraid of interjecting in a conversation when we are clearly struggling as we're trying to get our point across to someone.

Like, really, you can see our eyes screaming, "SAVE ME."

35. Always suggest staying in, ordering take-out and binge-watching on Netflix as an option instead of going out on the town in case we aren't feeling the nightlife.

We aren't hard to please kind of people. The less chaos, the better. We really truly enjoy these times with you much more than in a social setting.

36. When we tell you what we want to order before the waiter comes, then tell them what our order is for us.

We go ahead and tell you what we want so that you'll do this, and no one ever does! It would be so nice. Why should we have to speak to someone when you could just as easily do it for us? Please!

37. Take the time to acknowledge when we try really hard to be as calm, cool and collected as possible when we have to force ourselves to be a situation in which we'd rather not engage.

It takes a lot out of us to do this. Even if it's a simple, "thanks for trying today," that is more than enough for us.

38. Answer our phones for us when an unknown number calls or a number that we don't recognize.

The unknown makes us nervous. I mean, really nervous. Answering a call from an unknown number is like playing Russian Roulette for us.

39. If we make a mistake, then don't point it out to us harshly.

We can take constructive criticism but make sure it is worded correctly. One comment taken the wrong way can set off a tidal wave of questions and doubts about ourselves followed by the immense feeling of failure. "Fragile: Handle with Care."

40. Encourage us when we're feeling down.

Unfortunately, anxiety and depression pretty much go hand in hand. With fears and obsessions of failure comes the depressing thoughts that become obsessive, too. Make sure we know how you truly feel about it. Point out the positives when we are too far in the dark to see them.

41. When we are ready to talk about everything that's bothering us, please listen.

It takes a lot for us to finally open up and share our fears and insecurities that we know will sound trivial to anyone else, so when we are ready to express those things to you, don't take that lightly. All we really want is for someone to listen and to understand.

42. Don't let us go to bed confused or worried, if you can help it.

Your reassurance means more than you will ever know. If you are able to ease our minds, even in the slightest, then please try.

43. When we're feeling overwhelmed with things at home, offer to take over some of the chores.

Even if it's just doing the laundry, that's one less thing that's on our minds. We will be forever thankful for you to lighten our load. (no pun intended)

44. Encourage us to do whatever our hobbies we have that help to calm us.

Everyone has their own outlet that helps calms them and puts their thoughts to rest. Whether it's sketching, painting, writing, crocheting, listening to music, going for a jog, doing yoga, whatever it may be—encourage us to get back to things that make us happy and can settle our busy minds.

45. Make us feel safe in your presence.

We know that not everyone thinks the way that we do. We know that some things we think, say or do are irrational to some. All we want is a safe haven to be found in you, where we are loved and accepted. Always make us feel welcome to express our feelings and needs to you.

46. Stick with us through these trying times, even when we feel like we don't deserve you.

We are hard to live with. We know this. BUT WE ARE WORTH IT. Beneath the anxiety, we are passionate, caring people with every desire to love. If you can ride this out with us and find who we truly are away from the chaos, then you will be pleased that you did.

47. Inspire us to chase our dreams.

Our anxieties make us believe that if we ever try to achieve a goal that we have for ourselves, then there a million reasons why we will fail. We need you to push us to give it a shot, anyway. We need you to support us on our journey, and even if we do fail the first time, encourage us to try again because our happiness and fulfillment are worth it.

48. Talk to us about the favorite part of your day with us.

Since negativity fills our minds more times than not, we forget to focus on the good things that have happened. Remind us of what we did that made you happy to be there in that moment with us. Bring it to the light so we can see and cherish it with you.

49. Be our backbone when we have to face someone that is treating us poorly.

We can be quite the pushover because we tend to avoid confrontation. When you witness us being mistreated by a stranger or a friend alike, stand up for us. Remind us to stand up for ourselves because we don't deserve to be put down. Influence us to seek better for ourselves.

50. Most importantly, love us, even when we don't love ourselves.

That's all we want.

23

14 Things To Remember When You Love A Person With Anxiety

Koty Neelis

It wasn't until the past few years I realized how badly I suffered from anxiety. Simple things like waiting to hear back from someone or anticipating how something could turn out would leave my stomach in knots and my heart and mind racing. Now that I understand what anxiety is and how to help alleviate it, I understand a little bit better when I'm experiencing it. I don't pretend to know all the answers when it comes to anxiety or mental health, and I understand my experience isn't universal, but I hope these things can help anyone who loves someone else with anxiety and for the person with anxiety to realize they aren't alone.

1. It's not just all in their head and they can't just "get over" anxiety.

Over 40 million people have been diagnosed with an anxiety

disorder but those numbers don't report the other people who suffer with it every day without reporting it to their doctor. Anxiety is not something that can be cured with a simple "everything will be alright. there's nothing to worry about." The thing about anxiety is that nobody's entirely sure where it comes from or what causes it. The National Institute of Mental Health (NIMH) explains, "Panic disorder sometimes runs in families, but no one knows for sure why some people have it, while others don't."

2. Anxiety is an overwhelming experience.

Anxiety can leave a person feeling like their whole world is caving in. The first time I had a panic attack I was a teenager in a large shopping center with my mother. Suddenly, my mind was racing. I was sweating. The store suddenly felt very small and all of my senses were heightened. I felt like I was going to faint. My mom couldn't understand it and I couldn't understand it at the time either. We were just standing in an aisle while she was shopping for something. What was the problem?

When someone is experiencing anxiety, or when they suddenly have a panic attack, they get into a hyper-sense state where suddenly everything becomes very loud and very bright to them. The environment suddenly becomes a very overwhelming place.

3. Telling your loved one to "relax," "calm down," or

that something is "no big deal" doesn't help their anxiety. Sometimes, it only makes it worse.

When someone tells you they're worried or anxious about something, listen to what they're saying. Let them explain why something has them all at sea. Hear them out and try to understand from their point of view why they're feeling the way they do. It's understandable that people want to provide solutions or express to their loved one that whatever is causing them anxiety is actually not a huge deal, and it may not be, but in the moment when an anxious person is at the height of their emotion, telling them to relax only makes them feel like you're brushing aside something that is very real to them.

4. Not every anxious person is triggered by the same thing, and often, anxiety has no obvious triggers at all.

Something that's fun or enjoyable for you could have the complete opposite effect on someone with anxiety. For example, one of my anxiety triggers is being in large crowds. This is a problem for me because I love going to concerts and hearing live music.

A couple weeks ago I went to a music festival with a co-worker and in the middle of trying to leave after Drake performed, we were body to body with 50,000 people, all trying to leave the festival. We couldn't move and we were in a stand still. Immediately, my mind started racing, thinking about how this was a dangerous situation to be in, and about how many times I've heard of fatal incidences at music festivals where people were in this exact situation, and about how all I wanted was to get out and away from everyone. This was all going through my head, whereas my co-worker thought it was fun and awesome to be in the crowd with everyone.

Later, when I told one of my friends about it who has anxiety, she said, "Oh, interesting. Being around a lot of people doesn't bother me. It's when I'm faced with being in a one-on-one situation with someone, like if my friend randomly invites a new person to get drinks and leaves me alone with them, and then there's uncomfortable silence because I'm too awkward to make conversation—THAT'S what sends me into an instant panic until I have to excuse myself and go to the bathroom or escape the situation."

Basically, what I'm saying is, not every anxious person's experience is universal. We all experience anxiety differently, albeit in similar ways. Although someone can be self-aware of what factors seem to heighten their anxiety (drinking coffee, for example), there are no particular things you can predict that will engage a panic attack. They can come completely out of nowhere.

5. Sometimes they just need to be alone.

There are times when your loved one might decline to hang out over the weekend or with your friends so that they can be alone to decompress and just be by themselves. Try to remember to not take this personal. Remember their anxiety isn't a reflection on you or your relationship with them. People who deal with anxiety often just need more time to work things out in their head and think about everything going on in their life, especially if they've been particularly stressed lately.

6. They understand their fears can be irrational at times.

They know there are plenty of times when their anxiety makes absolutely no sense. Even if you both discuss the reality of the situation, their thought process is still thinking about the worse outcomes.

7. It can be difficult for them to let go of their fears.

Even if they've talked it all through and they rationally understand there's nothing to be anxious about, it can still be incredibly hard for them to let of the mindset there isn't something wrong.

8. If they open up to you about their anxiety, consider it a huge sign of trust.

One of the hardest parts of dealing with anxiety is feeling like you can't talk about it. The stigma that surrounds mental health is difficult to deal with because it makes those who have been diagnosed with a disorder feel like they're weird and shouldn't be open about their experience. If your loved one opens up to you about their anxiety, it's a sign they feel comfortable and open enough to you to be honest about a significant part of their life.

9. You won't always be able to tell when they're dealing with anxiety.

Just because someone is feeling extremely anxious, it doesn't mean they're going to be sitting there outwardly displaying signs of an anxious person. Many times people with anxiety suffer silently because they don't want to make a big deal out of something or because, well, it can be embarrassing to admit. There have been times where I've been at a party and a friend has told me quietly they needed to leave because they were feeling anxious. If they wouldn't have said anything I probably wouldn't have guessed anything was wrong.

Remember that even people who seem totally fine can be battling a war inside their mind.

10. You might not understand the ways they practice self-care.

Self-care is one of the most important things when going through a stressful time, and it's the little things that can make them feel better. Maybe it's doing a deep clean of the apartment or a closet, organizing books in a bookshelf by genre vs. alphabetical. You might think it's odd that the best way your loved one feels better is by cleaning the dishes, but many times these kind of activities are a form of meditation and help soothe the anxiety.

11. It's important you remember to practice your own self-care as well.

Just because the person you love deals with anxiety, it doesn't mean you have to walk on eggshells around them. They understand it can be a lot to deal with sometimes and they're grateful to have someone who cares about them. They don't expect you to forgive all of their flaws or mistakes—that's where patience and understanding are truly appreciated. But if things become too draining for you, you must also decide for yourself what your limits are in your relationship with them and where your boundaries lie. Whatever you do though, if at any point you think this person has too much baggage or too many issues for you, end it there. Don't lead them on into thinking you're someone they can count on.

12. Don't feel like it's up to you to solve all of their problems.

You and the love you give are not the solutions to your loved one's anxiety, but it can certainly aid as a balm. They don't expect you to solve something in their brain they don't even understand themselves and it's important to remember this so you don't feel burdened. Being someone that is simply there for them and listens to what they're going through can often be all they need to feel understood and cared for.

13. They need strong and stable relationships to truly thrive.

Relationships that are back and forth and fail to offer any real support, stability or longevity can make them feel unable to really connect with someone. They need their partner or loved one to keep them grounded and make them feel safe.

14. They might never be like anyone else—and that's okay!

Just because someone lives with anxiety, it doesn't mean that their anxiety defines them, and it isn't something that has to be seen as this great, overwhelming presence that dominates your connection with them. Be there for them. Listen to their fears, their concerns, their thoughts. Seek to understand and communicate. This person might not be like anyone else in your life but isn't that one of the most beautiful things about loving them?

24

This Is What Your Friend With Anxiety Actually Wants You To Say

Becca Martin

They don't want to hear you say, "calm down" or "it's all in your head" or "others have it worse than you." That's not helping, that's not comforting.

When you're struggling with anxiety you can't just "calm down" especially when you have anxiety over nothing, which is absolutely possible. And realistically the only thing you want when you have anxiety is to be calm. You want it all to go away and you want to feel normal, but it's not that easy because it's something you can't control.

Anxiety leaves you feeling helpless, it's like you're suffocating in your own body and you can't control it. You can tell yourself to breathe and calm down a million times, but it never works. Your brain doesn't understand how to calm down, the sickness you feel in your stomach and how completely uncomfortable you feel in your own body can't be controlled.

It's not in your head, it's real and it's happening. Being told everything is going to be okay doesn't immediately calm your nerves and settle your brain down from moving a million miles an hour. It's not something words can heal, but they can help if you say the right thing.

What they really need is support and encouragement; they need you to say, "I'm sorry you're going through this." Or "This must be really hard for you, let me know if there's anything I can do."

They need your support and your empathy. They need to know you're there for them just as an ear if they need to talk. They don't need you to tell them everything is going to be okay because things don't feel okay and realistically they probably won't be okay until their nerves have calmed drastically.

What your friend going through anxiety really needs is a connection.

They need to feel like you aren't trying to fix them because they aren't broken. They'll just want to be comforted by the fact that you're there for them.

Approaching them with an open mind and sensitivity is the key because that way they don't feel like they're being attacked or diminished. You'll help make them feel like they have someone there who isn't trying to diagnose them and tell them it's only small stuff they're getting worked up over because the truth is, they know it's the small stuff; they just can't control their emotions over it.

That's the thing about anxiety, no matter how irrelevant your problems seem to other people you can't just *make them disappear.*

Don't make their fears worse, but instead, help them through it. Be understanding and don't make their reasons behind their anxiety seem silly because to them it isn't. To them, it's causing them to be completely uncomfortable and alienated in their own body. It's a truly awful feeling.

The best things you can really do is just let them know you're there, tell them you're offering your support and let them know that you feel for them, that their worry isn't irrelevant and that they are welcomed to lean on you in times of need.

That's all they really want.

They want someone who understands, not someone who tries to fix them and change them.

Be empathetic and acknowledge their situation, that's what they want to hear because telling them to calm down will get them nowhere except more anxious.

25

Here's What You Need To Remember About Living With Anxiety

Nicole Vetrano

1. Anxiety is a mental illness and you should treat it like one.

Anxiety isn't just something you've made up in your head, but a mental illness that needs to be addressed and treated. This doesn't mean you need to immediately go on medication; it's not for everyone and acknowledging your anxiety as an illness doesn't mean that you're required to take pills.

But realizing that anxiety is an illness does help to validate the seriousness of the condition, something caused by a multitude of intricate and complex factors. Recognize that this isn't something you're overreacting about or have made up in your head.

2. Your anxiety is not your fault.

It's easy to blame yourself during periods of extreme anxiety.

Why am I like this? You may find yourself thinking. *Why can't I just be normal?*

What's so important to know is that the anxiety you experience is not your fault. You didn't cause this. You did nothing so horrible as for the universe to force this on you as a punishment.

The simple fact is that things happen in life that we can't control, so don't waste time beating yourself up about it. Positive outcomes occur when we learn to effectively deal with the situations that are, sometimes unfairly, thrust upon us.

Know that you haven't done anything wrong. Blaming yourself is only going to cause you to feel more anxious, so try to remind yourself that none of this is of your own doing.

3. Remember to breathe.

This may seem like something obvious, taking big deep breaths while in the midst of a panic attack, but it's easy to get caught up in the moment when you're experiencing bouts of anxiety. It's as much physical as it is mental, and it's important to understand that your mind is tricking your body into thinking you're in danger.

Try to remember to inhale deeply for three beats and exhale for just as long. Let your chest rise and fall in a rhythm. Feel the air expanding in your lungs. Allow for your racing heart to slow down to more of a normal pace through the breaths you take.

Remember that your anxiety is temporary and that it's impossible for it to last forever.

4. Find someone you can talk to.

Professionals are there for a reason and they're there to help. They understand the effects of anxiety, it's symptoms and the ways you can effectively deal with it. It's important to find someone you click with and feel comfortable around, but once you find that one person who can help you through it, I promise that it will be worth it the initial discomfort of spilling everything to a stranger.

But if paying someone to talk about your innermost issues isn't your thing, at least find someone you're close to who you feel you can trust and confide in. Surround yourself with positive people and stay away from those who choose not to understand.

5. You are not your stigma. Your anxiety does not define you.

All forms of mental illness come with some form of stigma attached to them and anxiety is no exception. People fear what they don't understand, and many don't realize the complex symptoms that anxiety can trigger in those plagued by it. People might assign judgements towards you based on your anxiety or make sweeping generalizations off of what they picture when they hear the word "anxiety."

Know that you are none of those things. You are not a caricature. You are not your circumstances. You are as much an individual as anyone else is in this world, no matter the preconceived notions that others may have.

Your anxiety may be a part of you, but it does not in any way define who you are. No matter what, you're going to be okay and know that it will not defeat you.

26

Read This If You Feel Like You're Losing The Battle With Your Anxiety

Bridget Kiely

Living with anxiety is a very tough reality for so many people. Some days are okay, some days are less okay, and some days you wake up with shaky hands and a racing mind. Some days your brain decides to remember every single awkward situation you've ever been in. Some days your muscles simply stop working, and you're stuck in bed thinking about your anxiety, but you can't do anything about it because you can't move. If you're having one of those days where the anxiety is just becoming too much, and you're not sure that you can make it to the end of the day, I'm here to tell you that you can and will get through it.

You need to remember that you will be okay.

You need to remember to breathe.

I know it's cliché and over-used and you probably don't think it will work, but it will. A deep breath can be so helpful in times of stress or anxiety. There is something so soothing about a deep breath. It's as if you're filling every single cell in your body with fresh air. It's as if your heart and brain are finally getting the message to slow down. It's the first thing you need to do to get that mind to stop racing.

You need to remember to talk about it.

So many people suffer from anxiety, but we never talk about it. Your feelings are real. Your problems are real. You can talk about it, and you should talk about it. I'm lucky enough to have a best friend who completely understands my anxiety. She knows how to calm me down and help me get through it. Talking to someone about my fears and feelings helps to get all of the ideas pinging around in my brain out into the open. It makes them feel like molehills, not mountains, and I know I can conquer a few molehills.

You need to remember to do something you love.

I find it way more difficult to feel anxious when I'm doing something I love. Even if I'm really busy, I make time to do things I love when I have bad days. It can be something as simple as watching an episode of your favorite TV show, or it can be something bigger like going to dinner with a friend or going to a concert. I know your brain is telling you to stay put and be worried, but doing something else to occupy your brain will get you out of that funk and back to being happy.

You need to remember to move.

Endorphins, endorphins, endorphins! Any doctor or psychologist will tell you that exercise is extremely important for your mental health. Endorphins themselves will make you feel better, but so will the sense of accomplishment from having had a great workout. If you're not a huge fan of the gym or running, do something different like hiking or even going for a walk. As long as you're moving, you're doing something to help yourself.

You need to remember to take a break.

I've noticed that I have really anxious days when I'm exhausted. I have a job that is physically and emotionally demanding, and that's something that is acknowledged by everyone I work with. We've been told that if we need a day off every once in a while just to get into a better headspace, we should take one. If I'm having one of those days when the world won't stop spinning and my hands won't stop shaking, I take a break. I unplug from social media and my phone and I take a day to watch movies, wear my pajamas, and get a grip on everything. Everyone needs to have do-nothing days every once in a while.

I know there are days when there doesn't seem to be a light at the end of the tunnel. There are days when you're drowning and no one can seem to help you to come up for air.

There are days when you feel so isolated and alone that the voices in your head have convinced you that things will never get better.

Anxiety is a very real and debilitating mental illness that makes you feel like there is no way you can ever get a handle on the world around you. You can. The wave will pass, the world will slow, and you'll come out on the other side stronger than ever before.

27

Why I Refuse to Let My Anxiety and Depression Define Me

Allison Case

Anxiety and depression. It is culminated in the constant thinking, worrying about everything, and letting it affect your life. The frustration, the self-loathing and the endless hours of time drowning in your own all-consuming thoughts.

I know it all because I've been there. Through every panic attack and mental breakdown alone in my room or in a room full of strangers, I've experienced it all. I can relate.

It's easy to feel like you're alone in it all. It's easy to convince yourself that you're not good enough for others because of your need to overanalyze every little thing. It's easy to sit helplessly as thoughts race through your head at a mile a minute every day. That's the problem with anxiety and depression; it makes it so easy for you to believe the worst when the world gives you every reason to celebrate.

Anxiety and depression can be crippling. It grasps your mind and body and doesn't let go, no matter how many times you convince yourself it doesn't, it can't, exist in you. It can make you feel weak and useless. But, you know what? It actually makes you the strongest person in the world.

Imagine waking up every morning to face the same issue day in and day out. You are doing just that, facing your own inner demons every single day. And it makes you stronger. Your anxiety and depression is making you stronger, no matter how much it feels like it is eating away at your insides and taking over your life.

Not only are you strong, but you are brave. You are brave for not simply giving in. You are brave for living your everyday life even though your mind is telling you that it is not worth the pain. And anxiety and depression can be painful to the point where you feel the need to hole up in your room and let the tears spill out. Crying out the frustration becomes more appealing when your mind is constantly running at the speed of light, telling you you're not worthy of all the good things life has to offer.

The demons you have to face are ones that live inside of you, and how brave are you to deal with them every minute of every day?

Even worse, it becomes so simple to look at others and compare yourself to them. Magnified by anxiety and depression, comparing myself to the world around me is a common practice in my daily routine. I want to stop, but sometimes my mind insists on rehashing everything I don't have and never will have.

There are times when I look in the mirror and hate what I see. My mind is constantly telling me to be skinnier, prettier and just better. And guess what? You'll believe it because who do you trust more than yourself? It is a never-ending cycle of thoughts that can keep you awake all night long. But it's not just you.

Sometimes you feel embarrassed or ashamed, but anxiety and depression is something so common. Millions of people go through the same thing each and every day and they understand. The last thing you are in this world is alone in your fight against yourself.

It is time for us to stop feeling embarrassed for being in our own heads. There historically has been a stigma associated with anxiety and depression, but the more people talk about it, the more that stigma will end up becoming the norm.

They always say God gives his hardest battles to his toughest soldiers and this...this is tough. There's nothing worse than feeling like you aren't even good enough for yourself, let alone others.

Overcoming this won't be easy or an overnight fix. But that is okay. And you need to remember that.

Each day that you get up and go on with life is a day that you've won the battle. Each day you take on the world is a little victory.

So, do one thing that scares you each day. Be brave. Because as those small victories become the norm, you'll begin to realize that anxiety and depression may be a part of your life, but they certainly don't define it.

28

37 Freeing Quotes For People With Anxiety

Chrissy Stockton

1. P.S. You're not going to die. Here's the white-hot truth: if you go bankrupt, you'll still be okay. If you lose the gig, the lover, the house, you'll still be okay. If you sing off-key, get beat by the competition, have your heart shattered, get fired…it's not going to kill you. Ask anyone who's been through it.

—Daneille LaPorte

2. If you obsess over whether you are making the right decision, you are basically assuming that the universe will reward you for one thing and punish you for another. The universe has no fixed agenda. Once you make any decision, it works around that decision. There is no right or wrong, only a series of possibilities that shift with each thought, feeling, and action that you experience.

—Deepak Chopra

3. I promise you nothing is as chaotic as it seems. Nothing is worth your health. Nothing is worth poisoning yourself into stress, anxiety, and fear.

—*Steve Maraboli*

4. Anxiety's like a rocking chair. It gives you something to do, but it doesn't get you very far.

—*Jodi Picoult*

5. Some of us think holding on makes us strong, but sometimes it is letting go.

—*Hermann Hesse*

6. It's not stress that kills us, it is our reaction to it.

—*Hans Selye*

7. Anxiety is a thin stream of fear trickling through the mind. If encouraged, it cuts a channel into which all other thoughts are drained.

—*Arthur Somers Roche*

8. Don't let your mind bully your body into believing it must carry the burden of its worries.

—*Astrid Alauda*

9. My need to solve the problem is the problem.

—*Unknown*

10. Every time you are tempted to react in the same old way, ask if you want to be a prisoner of the past or a pioneer of the future.

—*Deepak Chopra*

11. Nothing in the universe can stop you from letting go and starting over.

—*Guy Finley*

12. Smile, breathe, and go slowly.

—*Thich Nhat Hanh*

13. Don't try to steer the river.

—*Deepak Chopra*

14. Stress is caused by being 'here' but wanting to be 'there.'

—*Eckhart Tolle*

15. Worrying is carrying tomorrow's load with today's strength—carrying two days at once. It is moving into tomorrow ahead of time. Worrying doesn't empty tomorrow of its sorrow, it empties today of its strength.

—*Corrie ten Boom*

16. Nothing is permanent in this wicked world—not even our troubles.

—*Charlie Chaplin*

17. Every day brings a choice: to practice stress or to practice peace.

—*Joan Borysenko*

18. Anxiety is one little tree in your forest. Step back and look at the whole forest.

—*Unknown*

19. There must be quite a few things that a hot bath won't cure, but I don't know many of them.

—*Sylvia Plath*

20. God didn't do it all in one day. What makes me think I can?

—*Unknown*

21. Let yourself be open and life will be easier. A spoon of salt in a glass of water makes the water undrinkable. A spoon of salt in a lake is almost unnoticed.

—*Buddha*

22. Abundance is a process of letting go; that which is empty can receive.

—*Bryant H. McGill*

23. People have a hard time letting go of their suffering. Out of a fear of the unknown, they prefer suffering that is familiar.

—*Thich Nhat Hanh*

24. If you gathered up all the fearful thoughts that exist in the mind of the average person, looked at them objectively, and tried to decide just how much good they provided that person, you would see that not some but all fearful thoughts are useless. They do no good. Zero. They interfere with dreams, hopes, desire, and progress.

—*Richard Carlson*

25. You cannot make yourself feel something you do not feel, but you can make yourself do right in spite of your feelings.

—*Pearl S. Buck*

26. As a doctor, let me tell you what self-love does: It improves your hearing, your eyesight, lowers your blood pressure, increases pulmonary function, cardiac output, and helps wiring the musculature. So, if we had a rampant epidemic of self-love then our healthcare costs would go down dramatically. So, this isn't just some little frou-frou new age notion, oh love yourself honey. This is hardcore science.

—*Dr. Christiane Northrop*

27. Stress is the trash of modern life—we all generate it but if you don't dispose of it properly, it will pile up and overtake your life.

—*Terri Guillemets*

28. Sometimes people let the same problem make them miserable for years when they could just say, So what. That's one of my favorite things to say. So what.

—*Andy Warhol*

29. We must be willing to let go of the life we've planned, so as to have the life that is waiting for us.

—*Joseph Campbell*

30. Said the river to the seeker, "Does one really have to fret about enlightenment? No matter which way I turn, I'm homeward bound."

—*Anthoney De Mello*

31. Because believing that the dots will connect down the road will give you the confidence to follow your heart even when it leads you off the well-worn path.

—*Steve Jobs*

32. I know but one freedom and that is the freedom of the mind.

—*Antoine de Saint-Exupery*

33. The greatest weapon against stress is our ability to choose one thought over another.

—*William James*

34. You forgive yourself for every failure because you are trying to do the right thing. God knows that and you know it. Nobody else may know it.

—*Maya Angelou*

35. Be soft. Do not let the world make you hard. Do not let pain make you hate. Do not let the bitterness steal your sweetness. Take pride that even though the rest of the world may disagree, you still believe it to be a beautiful place.

—*Kurt Vonnegut*

36. You can only lose what you cling to.

—*Buddha*

37. When I let go of what I am, I become what I might be. When I let go of what I have, I receive what I need.

—*Tao Te Ching*

15 Signs You're Being Too Hard On Yourself

Rania Naim

1. You can't celebrate your success because you think that there's still more to accomplish or that you're not as successful as you should be.

2. You blame yourself for every bad thing that happened in your life without considering external factors or other people involved.

3. When you examine yourself, you only see your flaws and your shortcomings and feel incompetent.

4. You still have a lot of regrets from the past that you can't get over or let go of and you're always imagining how your life would be if you made wiser or better decisions.

5. You feel like you don't deserve unconditional love because you're struggling to love yourself and you don't see why anyone would either.

6. It's harder for you to accept compliments or praise because you're always thinking about how far you still need to go instead of how far you've come.

7. You're scared of opening up to people or letting people in because you don't think anyone will stay with you once they get to know the *real* you.

8. You're always doing things for people and overwhelming yourself because you feel guilty when you say no and you think people will hold it against you.

9. Because you always want to be better or more accomplished, you don't always feel good enough about yourself and it takes a toll on your self-esteem.

10. You don't know how to be kind to yourself. You don't know how to relax, how to praise yourself, how to give yourself a pat on the back or how to *forgive* yourself.

11. You tend to worry too much and think of the worst outcome for a situation because your mind is programmed to pick the hardest battle.

12. You give people a chance to mistreat you or criticize you a lot because you're already self-critical so when someone confirms it in any way, you don't really stand up for yourself.

13. You have trouble sleeping at night because you over think everything, which is why you're always fatigued or cranky.

14. You think being hard on yourself pushes you forward but it's actually holding you back because you can't appreciate the good things about you and you hold on to the thoughts that bring you down.

15. Sometimes you expect people to be hard on you too, so you let them get away with hurting you.

30

Just So You Know, Some Day You're Going To Be Okay

Alexandria Brown

I want to be the girl everyone thinks I am.

The one who's taken on the world without any sort of issue. The one who stands up for everything she believes in. The girl who has managed to change sceneries time and time again without even batting an eyelash. I want to be the girl in my photos who's smiling or laughing with different people in different places.

I don't want to be the girl who's currently covered under her duvet wondering when everything got to a point of no return. I don't want to be the girl who's been under such stress from her own depression and anxiety that she's had to move back home. The girl who's had trouble admitting to herself that things aren't going well. That everything that's been going on lately has been way too much for her to shoulder on her own.

I want to be the girl that used to have everything come so naturally and easy that it looked so effortless.

Life doesn't work that way, though. If there's one thing I've learned over the last 26 years of being on this Earth is that at one point or another we're all going to struggle. Some of us will struggle privately and manage to pull ourselves out of our darkest moments.

Some of us will realize that there comes a time and point when we need to lean on all the people who love us wholeheartedly for extra love during times of despair.

The older I get the more I realize that we're so scared to talk about when we're going through the really bad lows. That is largely due to the new normal of being flawless on social media. We look at everyone else's lives that are going perfectly and compare them to our own. Comparison is natural but we shouldn't compare ourselves to such extreme points that it makes us question our own worth.

I find my default is comparing my older self to my younger self. I look back at 21 and think about how back then I was drinking way too much, dating really shitty guys and ignoring all of the mental health warning flags that kept appearing. I didn't give a shit about being unhealthy because I didn't have time to care about myself. I was too busy trying to find my worth at the bottom of a bottle or on the other side of some loser's bed. To me, though, in those moments of comparison, everything is idealized and romanticized. I only see the good.

I can logically look at those situations now and see the

imperfections within them. I can see the damaging behavior I had allowed into my life daily.

I can see the fact that those decisions I made back then have made me who I am today.

While I wouldn't change any experience I've had, I just wish I had been honest with myself back then. Maybe then I wouldn't be the girl who's holed up in her bedroom trying to figure out how to feel happiness again.

It's *scary* to stand here with my chest open and all my feelings spilling out of me like I don't have any time to catch them. It's *scary* to admit that my depression has hit such a low that my life has now been altered in major ways. It's *scary* to think that from here on out I'm probably not going to be the same person anymore.

We get caught up in the fact that there will be people who turn their backs on you when you start getting real about your mental illness. We start to worry that the judgments are going to be worse that silently struggling through the day. We don't want to start being handled like we're breakable. While I know that the only thing that should matter is getting better, I also am well aware of how it feels to be belittled for having anxiety and depression.

So while you're sitting at home, trying to figure out if you should keep on pretending that you're OK or if you should reach out to someone close to you to tell them that right now you're not sure how to keep it together. **My advice is this; it's** always better to deal with it head on than to let it fester. Fuck anyone who thinks you're weak because of your mental illness.

You are brave. You are strong. You will find your happiness again. All you need to do is put yourself first and other's opinions last.

Thought Catalog, it's a website.

www.thoughtcatalog.com

Social

facebook.com/thoughtcatalog

twitter.com/thoughtcatalog

tumblr.com/thoughtcatalog

instagram.com/thoughtcatalog

Corporate

www.thought.is

Made in the USA
Columbia, SC
03 December 2019